C000053237

A vast and sprawling metropolis with no real center, daringly avant-garde and yet so traditional, London is a capital like no other. It grew up around the City, its commercial center, and Westminster, the seat of power and headquarters of the Anglican religion. Gradually, surrounding villages were absorbed into the urban fabric, unifying it and giving rise to the Londoners' love of green open spaces, whether small domestic gardens or enormous parks where one goes riding or comes to watch performances of Shakespeare in leafy open-air theaters. Those former villages have left a heritage of interlocking districts, each with its own distinctive personality: St James's with its art galleries; the West End with its theaters, and ever-partying Soho; literary Bloomsbury, artistic Chelsea, royal Kensington, bohemian Notting Hill. Further out, Islington, Clerkenwell and the now trend-setting East End have long been drawn into the rambling city landscape. London is fond of its old-fashioned traditions but this cosmopolitan city is also a place where things happen first, and its continental counterparts watch closely. New trends spring up everywhere: in a street market, in a designer's window, in a music bar or on the dance floor of a nightclub. There's no time to lose: come and discover all the magic London has to offer with this MapGuide.

Find your bearings in London

A Westminster / Whitehall

B Covent Garden / Soho / Bloomsbury

C City / St Paul's / Shoreditch / Clerkenwell

D Islington / King's Cross / Camden / Hampstead

E Mayfair / Marylebone

F Kensington / Notting Hill

G Chelsea / South Kensington / Belgravia

H South Bank / Waterloo

I Southwark / Tower Bridge

J Docklands / Greenwich / East End

HAMPSTEAD HEATH

CRICKLEWOOD LA

HENDON WAY

EDGWARE ROAD

WILLESDEN LANE

D HAMPSTEAD

KENTISH TOWN ROAD

BROADWAY SHOOT UP HILL

ST JOHN'S WOOD

PRIMROSE HILL

CAMDEN MARKETS

CA

A205

HARROW ROAD

MAIDA VALE

E WELLINGTON HOSPITAL

REGENT'S PARK

EUS STAT

LITTLE VENICE

WESTWAY

B

F PADDINGTON

WESTWAY

PADDINGTON STATION

MARYLEBONE WALLACE COLLECTION

WEST

PORTOBELLO ROAD MARKET

OXFORD ST

NOTTING HILL ✪

BAYSWATER

BAYSWATER RD

HYDE PARK ✪

MAYFAIR

NATI GAL

KENSINGTON GARDENS ✪

SERPENTINE

BUCKINGHAM PALACE

KENSINGTON PALACE

HOLLAND PARK

ROYAL ALBERT HALL

KNIGHTSBRIDGE ✪

WESTMIN

KENSINGTON

NATURAL HISTORY MUSEUM

VICTORIA & ALBERT MUSEUM

VICTORI STATIO

PIMLIC

A

SOUTH KENSINGTON

EARL'S COURT

CHELSEA

HAMMERSMITH

WEST BROMPTON

BATTERSEA PARK

G

FULHAM

BATTERSEA

BATTERSEA PARK

FULHAM PALACE RD

FULHAM RD

A304

R. THAMES

HURLINGHAM PARK

PUTNEY HIGH ST

ST JOHN'S HILL

TRINITY ROAD

CLA

CLAPHAM COMMON LONG ROAD

CLAPHAM COMMON

CAVENDISH ROAD

0   1   2 km

1/ 100 000 - 1 cm = 1 km

Top ten

London sights you should not miss

✪ National Gallery (A C1**)**
Around 2,000 pictures present an unrivaled overview of European art. Housed in a fine neoclassical building (1838) the gallery displays its collection chronologically in a series of rooms from the 13th to the 19th centuries, from the Italian Primitives to French Impressionism, passing through the Flemish and Spanish schools. The National Portrait Gallery next door has pictures of famous Britons from Henry VIII to present-day personalities.

✪ Westminster (A D3**)**
The view of the Houses of Parliament with its clock tower housing Big Ben, and the Abbey nearby, is a microcosm of English history. The former was built on the site of the 11th-century Palace of Westminster between 1840 and 1888, while the latter has been the setting for royal coronations and funerals since William the Conqueror in 1066. Handel, Dickens, Kipling, Tennyson and Hardy are among the great men buried in the Abbey.

✪ The British Museum (B C2**)**
Ancient Egypt, the Near East, Greek and Roman antiquities, primitive art... it would take weeks to see everything on display in this dazzling museum that has over six million objects from civilizations all over the world. It was founded in 1753, based on the collections of Dr Hans Sloane (1660–1753) and expanded so rapidly that its contents later formed the basis of two other great institutions: the Natural History Museum (**G** B2) in 1881, and the British Library (**D** D3) in 1997.

✪ Tate Britain (A D5**)** and **Tate Modern (I** A1**)**
Opened in 1897 thanks to wealthy tycoon Sir Henry Tate, the museum has finally fulfilled its original purpose: to display a vast collection of British painting along with great works of modern art. Converted from a fomer power station in 2000 by Herzog and de Meuron and having undergone a spectacular expansion in 2016, Tate Modern fulfils the second role; and the Millbank Gallery, renamed Tate Britain, is dedicated to the national art heritage, including 300 canvases by J. M. W. Turner (1775–1851). The two galleries are linked by a ferry-boat (Tate-to-Tate).

✪ The City / St Paul's Cathedral (C C3**)**
As well as being London's financial district, the City is also the site of the original metropolis, its boundaries being those of the Roman Londinium, founded in the 1st century. Swarming with business people by day, the City becomes eerily quiet on weekends, when only tourists come to see the many fine churches that remain in the area. All converge onto the most famous, St Paul's Cathedral, Christopher Wren's masterpiece. Climb up the 528 steps to the Golden Gallery for stunning panoramic views of the capital.

✪ Hyde Park (E B6**) and Kensington Gardens (F** E3**)**
Separated only by the Serpentine (an artificial lake), these two parks comprise over 700 acres of green open space in the heart of London. Hyde Park has been popular ever since it was first opened to the public by King Charles I (1625–49). Kensington Gardens, lying on the west side of the lake, were formerly the grounds of Kensington Palace, to which Queen Anne added the Orangery in 1704.

✪ Notting Hill (F B2**)**
Originally farmland up to the 1870s, then a chic residential area, Notting Hill became strikingly cosmopolitan in the 1950s when immigrants from the Caribbean began settling here. This fashionable district is worth seeing for its market on Portobello Road, its amazing annual street carnival, and the host of fashion boutiques lining Westbourne Grove, Ledbury Road and the small streets around.

✪ Victoria & Albert Museum (G C2**)**
The world's greatest museum of arts and design, the V&A displays furniture, jewelry, fabrics, costume, ceramics and much more, dating back over 2,000 years. Don't miss *Tippoo's Tiger*, a famous automaton, or the *Great Bed of Ware* (*c.*1600) that can sleep up to 15 people.

✪ Tower of London / Tower Bridge (I E1 **/** F1**)**
With a maze of towers and passageways inside its massive walls, the 11th-century royal fortress has been the scene of many bloodthirsty events and a magnet for sightseers since the reign of Queen Victoria (1837–1901). Next to the Tower is Tower Bridge, built at the end of the 19th century, which still opens today to allow shipping to pass through.

✪ Changing of the Guard at Buckingham Palace (A A3**)**
Through the railings of Buckingham Palace, crowds come to watch the guards carry out this daily ritual dressed in their scarlet tunics and black bearskin hats. The ceremony takes place daily at 11.30am when guard duty is switched from one regiment to another to the sound of a fanfare. A must for the first-time visitor. *Note: takes place on alternate days between August and March*

CITY PROFILE

- The largest city in Britain and in Europe
- 610 square miles
- 8.5 million inhabitants in Greater London
- 26 million visitors every year
- More than 300 languages spoken
- The Thames flows 40 miles through the city
- Gets its name from the Roman settlement *Londinium*, where the current 'City of London' stands. This is the financial district, which is often referred to as the 'square mile', demarcated as it is by its medieval boundaries

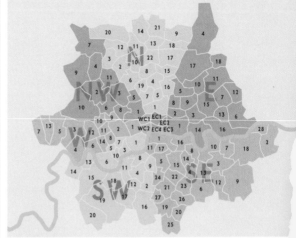

LONDON DISTRICTS

WWW.

→ visitlondon.com
The official website of the London Tourist Office.
→ londontown.com
→ viewlondon.co.uk
Addresses of restaurants, bars, movie theaters, pubs.
→ visitbritain.com

TOURIST INFO

City of London Information Centre (**C** C3)
→ St Paul's Churchyard, EC4
Mon-Sat 9.30am–5.30pm;
Sun 10am–4pm
There are also tourist information points at many large train stations.

TELEPHONE

USA to London
→ 011 + 44 (UK) + number, omitting the initial 0
London to the USA
→ 00 + 1 (USA) + number

Within London
→ 020 + eight-digit number starting with 7 or 8
Useful numbers
Police, fire, ambulance
→ Tel. 999 or 112 (cell phones)
Operator
→ 100 national
→ 155 international
Lost Property (**E** B2)
→ 200 Baker St, NW1
Tel. 0845 330 9882
Mon-Fri 8.30am–4pm

DIARY OF EVENTS

Public holidays
→ Jan 1 (New Year's Day);
Good Friday; Easter Monday;
first Mon in May; last Mon in
May; last Mon in Aug; Dec 25;
Dec 26 (Boxing Day)
January-February
New Year's Eve Parade
→ Jan 1
London Intl Mime Festival
→ 3 weeks in Feb
mimelondon.com
Celebration of contemporary visual

theater with shows at venues around the city.
Chinese New Year
→ End Jan-beg Feb; in
Trafalgar Square, Leicester
Square and Chinatown
Parades, markets, etc.
Pancake Race
→ One Tue in Feb or March
Race in which participants flip pancakes in a pan as they run.
March
St Patrick's Day
→ March 17
Celebrations in honour of Ireland's patron saint.
The Boat Race
→ Sun, end March-beg April
Famous race on the Thames: Oxford vs Cambridge University.
April-May
London Marathon
→ One Sun in April
Around 30,000 runners.
Chelsea Flower Show
→ Third or fourth week in May
At the Royal Hospital (**G** E3).
Museums at Night

→ few days in May & Oc
Explore history, art and heritage after dark at museums and gallerie across the city.
Clerkenwell Design Week
→ Three days end May
80 showrooms around Clerkenwell showcase the latest in furniture and product design.
June
Trooping the Colour
→ Second Sat; Horse
Guards Parade (**A** C2)
Military parade on the Queen's birthday.
Derby Day, Royal Ascot
→ Early June
Famous horse races.
City of London Festival
→ Mid June-mid July
colf.org
Varied, world-class music, dance and theater performances around the city; free of charge.
Wimbledon
→ Late June-early July

FIND YOUR BEARINGS

London has 33 boroughs – the main subdivisions of the Greater London area – each governed by a London borough council. Twelve are designated as Inner London and 20 as Outer London (the 33rd is the City of London).

Getting around
The boroughs are divided into districts identified by postcodes (EC=East Central, N= North, SW=South West etc). As a rule, the higher the number of the district, the further it is from the city center.

PRIMROSE HILL TERRACES

PORTOBELLO ROAD

One of the four Grand Slam tournaments.
July-August
Proms
→ *Mid July-mid Sep*
bbc.co.uk/proms
Classical music concerts at the Royal Albert Hall (**G** B1).
Notting Hill Carnival
→ *Last weekend in Aug*
Caribbean street festival on Portobello Road (**F** B2).
Coin Street Festival (**H** C2)
→ *One w/e in June and July*
Free cultural events in the open air, on the South Bank.
Swan Upping on the Thames
→ *One week in July*
Dating from the 12th century, a census of the swans on the Thames.
Great British Beer Festival
→ *Five days in Aug*
For a taste of traditional British beers.
September-October
Totally Thames Festival
→ *Sep; totallythames.org*

Boats on the Thames, street theater, fireworks.
London Open House
→ *Third weekend in Sep*
Visit buildings usually closed to the public.
BFI London Film Festival
→ *Ten days in Oct*
bfi.org.uk/lff
International film festival on the South Bank (**H** B2)
Frieze Art Fair
→ *Four days in Oct*
Contemporary art fair in Regent's Park.
November-December
London Jazz Festival
→ *10 days in November*
efglondonjazzfestival.org.uk
Over 300 concerts in approximately 50 venues across the city.
Lord Mayor's Show
→ *Second Sat in Nov*
lordmayorsshow.org
Procession for the election of the Lord Mayor.
Christmas tree and lights
→ *Mid Nov-early Jan*
Illuminations on Oxford

St (**E** C4) and Regent St (**E** D4); and the mounting of the largest Christmas tree in the city in Trafalgar Square (**A** C1).

BUDGET

Accommodation
A basic double room en suite in the city center: £90–120.
Eating out
A main course in a standard restaurant: £11–20; fish & chips: £7–13.
Sightseeing
Entry to a museum: free–£15; to attractions and major sites: £15–30.
Going out
A beer: £4; entry to a movie theater: £9–15; entry to a club: £6–20.
London for less
International student card
→ *isic.tm.fr*
London Pass
→ *£55 (1 day)–£121 (6 days); £68–164 inc. unlimited travel*

ARCHITECTURE

Gothic style
Between the 12th and 15th c., increasing use of sculpture and stained glass, for a more 'ornate' Gothic; Westminster Abbey (**A** D3)
Tudor style (1485–1603)
High fan vaulting for churches, red brick and surbased arches or Flemish-style stud work for private residences; Lady Chapel, Westminster Abbey (**A** D3)
Baroque (17th–18th c.)
This period, marked by the Great Fire of 1666, is dominated by a restrained baroque, despite a richness of details, especially in Wren's work; St Paul's Cathedral (**C** C3)
Georgian style (1714–1830)
Symmetrical buildings with noble white stone façades and colonnades inspired by antiquity; Belgrave Square (**G** E1)
Victorian era (1837–1901)
Gothic Revival and a return to red-brick houses; Houses of Parliament (**A** D3). During the industrial era, huge metallic structures sprung up everywhere; Leadenhall Market (**C** E3)
Contemporary London
Rebuilding of the city after the Blitz using mainly concrete. Financial buildings spring up in the 1980s. High-tech 21st-century projects inclue Swiss Re Tower (**C** E3), 20 Fenchurch St (**C** C4), The Shard (**I** D2)

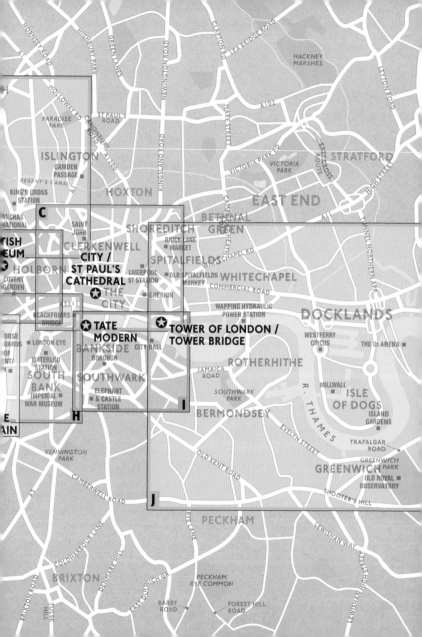

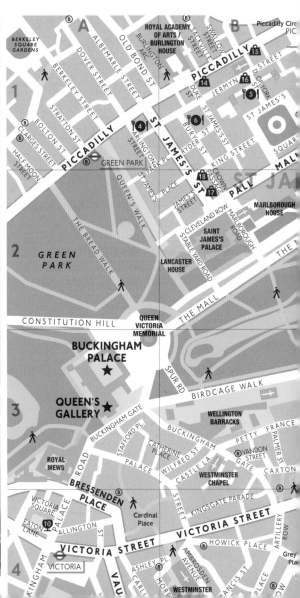

NATIONAL GALLERY

NATIONAL PORTRAIT GALLERY

TRAFALGAR SQUARE /
NELSON'S COLUMN

BERKELEY
SQUARE
GARDENS

A

ROYAL ACADEMY
OF ARTS /
BURLINGTON
HOUSE

B

Piccadilly Circ
PIC

ALBEMARLE STREET

OLD BOND ST

BURLINGTON ARC

SACKVILLE
STREET

SWALLOW
STREET

PICCADILLY

15

DOVER STREET

14

JERMYN ST

16

5

DUKE ST

ST JAMES'S ST

BURY ST

6

ST JAMES'S

BOLTON ST

STRATTON ST

ARLINGTON
STREET

4

ST JAMES'S ST

RYDER ST

KING STREET

SQUAR

BERKELEY STREET

PICCADILLY

GREEN PARK

QUEEN'S WALK

ST JAMES'S PLACE

CROWN
PASSAGE

18

17

PALL

MAL

ST JA

CLARGES STREET

HALF MOON
STREET

QUEEN'S WALK

JAMES'S
STREET

CLEVELAND ROW

MARLBOROUGH
ROAD

MARLBOROUGH
HOUSE

THE N

THE BREAD WALK

GREEN
PARK

SAINT JAMES'S
PALACE

STABLE YARD ROAD

LANCASTER
HOUSE

2

THE MALL

CONSTITUTION HILL

QUEEN
VICTORIA
MEMORIAL

BUCKINGHAM
PALACE ★

SPUR RD

BIRDCAGE WALK

QUEEN'S ★
GALLERY

3

BUCKINGHAM GATE

STAFFORD PL.

CATHERINE
PLACE

BUCKINGHAM

WILFRED ST

CASTLE LA.

WELLINGTON
BARRACKS

PETTY
FRANCE

VANDON
STREET

PALMER ST

CAXTON

ROYAL
MEWS

ROAD

PALACE

WESTMINSTER
CHAPEL

BRESSENDEN
PLACE

VICTORIA
SQUARE

PALACE

EATON
LANE

ALLINGTON ST

10

Cardinal
Place

STREET

KINGSGATE PARADE

VICTORIA STREET

VICTORIA STREET

HOWICK PLACE

ARTILLERY
ROW

4

VICTORIA

ASHLEY PL.

AMBROSDEN
AVENUE

CARL

MOR

WESTMINSTER

FRANCIS ST

PLACE

OW

Grey
Pla

Trafalgar Square opens out onto two imposing avenues, The Mall and Whitehall, both of which are lined with prominent symbols of political and religious power: the royal residence, ministries, churches and the seat of government at Westminster. The upmarket men's stores on St James and Jermyn Streets are equally refined. Once past Victoria Tower Gardens, narrow streets bordered by 18th-century façades wind their way around Smith Square. Further south, residential areas built mainly in the Victorian period radiate a tranquil aura which gradually evaporates the closer you get to Victoria Station.

AL DUCA

GORDON'S WINE BAR

RESTAURANTS

Cellarium Cafe (D3) ▯❶▯
→ 20 Dean's Yard, SW1
Tel. 020 7222 0516
Mon-Fri 8am–6pm; Sat 9am–5pm; Sun 10am–4pm
Cross the cloister of Westminster Abbey, go down into the impressive Gothic cellar and relish the appetizing breakfasts and creative salads on offer. Entrées £7–17.

Giraffe (A5) ▯❷▯
→ 120 Wilton Road, SW1
Tel. 020 7233 8303
Mon-Fri 8am–11pm; Sat-Sun 9am–11pm (10.30pm Sun)
Food for all the family in a cheerful setting: mezze, burgers, sandwiches, falafel and grilled corn on the cob. Entrées £9–16.

The National Dining Rooms (C1) ▯❸▯
→ National Gallery, Sainsbury Wing, Trafalgar Square, WC2
Tel. 020 7747 2525; Daily 10am–5.30pm (8.30pm Fri)
Traditional English food served in the National Gallery, underneath a Renaissance fresco: braised kidneys, cockle soup, regional cheeses. Next door, the National Café and Grab and Go serve breakfasts and fresh snacks. Entrées £14–21.50.

The Wolseley (A1) ▯❹▯
→ 160 Piccadilly, W1
Tel. 020 7499 6996
Daily noon–3pm (3.30pm Sat-Sun), 5.30pm–midnight (11pm Sun)
A splendid, high-ceilinged 1920s building resembling a Viennese brasserie, with gold-and-black decor and a chequerboard marble floor. Good brasserie-type food and afternoon tea. Impeccable service. Entrées £14–32.

Al Duca (B1) ▯❺▯
→ 4-5 Duke of York St, SW1
Tel. 020 7839 3090
Mon-Fri noon–11pm; Sat 12.30–11pm
Excellent seasonal Italian cuisine and homemade pasta in a smart dining room. Prix fixe (dinner) £29.50; entrées £13–18.

Matsuri (B1) ▯❻▯
→ 15 Bury St, SW1
Tel. 020 7839 1101; Daily noon–2.30pm, 6–10.30pm
Japanese cuisine raised to an art form, with sublime sushi and sashimi. Teppanyaki downstairs, where chefs show off their impressive knife skills. Impeccable service. Prix fixe £16 (lunch)–£165 (dinner).

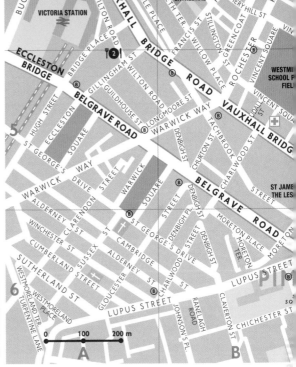

HORSE GUARDS

BUCKINGHAM PALACE

★ **National Portrait Gallery** (C1)
→ *St Martin's Place, WC2 Tel. 020 7306 0055; Daily 10am–6pm (9pm Thu-Fri)*
A wonderful history of Britain in pictures, with more than 9,000 portraits (paintings, etchings, drawings and photographs) of statesmen, musicians, writers and artists, from Nicholas Hilliard's portrait of Elizabeth I in 1572, to that of the former Mayor of London, Ken Livingstone.

★ **National Gallery** (C1)
→ *Trafalgar Square, WC2 Daily 10am–6pm (9pm Fri)*
Founded in 1824 with the acquisition of 38 pictures

from the banker John Julius Angerstein, the gallery houses one of the world's best European painting collections from the 13th to the 19th centuries. Famous pieces include the *Pentecost* by Giotto, *Pope Julius II* by Raphael, *The Ambassadors* by Holbein, the *Sunflowers* by Van Gogh and *A Young Woman Standing at a Virginal* by Vermeer.

★ **Trafalgar Square / Nelson's Column** (C1)
In 2003 the north of the square conceived by John Nash (1752–1835) was pedestrianized, and a staircase links the now traffic-free area, in front

of the National Gallery, with the square below. At its center is the 185-ft-high column dedicated to the British naval hero Admiral Nelson (1758–1805). The bronze bas-reliefs on the base were made from cannons seized during Nelson's victories over the French and Spanish fleets at the Battle of Trafalgar in 1805.

★ **Horse Guards** (D2)
→ *Whitehall, SW1 Changing of the Guards daily 11am (10am Sun)*
Four imperturbable guards mounted on superb horses and wearing distinctive bearskin hats are posted

in front of the barracks of the Royal Guard. The esplanade on the side of St James's Park is the best vantage point.

★ **Buckingham Palace** (A3)
→ *The Mall, SW1 Tel. 020 7766 7300; Aug-Se 9.15am–7.45pm (6.45pm S Changing of the Guard: da 11.30am (every two days Aug-March); Royal Mews: Mar, Nov: Mon-Sat 10am–4 April–Oct: Daily 10am–5pm*
The home of the British monarchy since Queen Victoria took up residen here in 1837. It is only op to visitors in the summe but the Changing of the

THE THAMES, TOWER BRIDGE AND THE CANARY WHARF TOWERS SEEN FROM THE SHARD

PUBS

11pm...last orders!
A compulsory closing time was imposed in 1915 to boost the war effort, and in a number of pubs a bell still rings at 10.50pm for last orders.

Gastropubs
Boundaries between bar, pub and restaurant became blurred when certain pubs sparked off a revival of English cuisine by reintroducing high-quality classic dishes to their menus. The term 'gastropub' is synonymous today with good food in relaxed surroundings.

on public transport
Free entry to 56 sites plus discounts.

TKTS kiosk (B C4)
→ *Leicester Sq.; Mon-Sat 9am–7pm; Sun 11am–4pm*
Half-price seats for same day plays and musicals.

londonforfree.net
Things to do in the capital for free, or for very little money.

National museums
Most of them are free.

OPENING HOURS

Museums
→ *Usually daily 10am–6pm (incl. Sun and public hols)*
Restaurants
→ *Usually noon–3pm, 6–10.30pm (last orders)*
Pubs
→ *Usually 11am–11pm/ midnight (some later)*
Nightclubs
→ *Most close around 3am (6am on the weekend)*
Shops

→ *Usually Mon-Sat 9/10am– 6pm (later on Thu); most are open Sun noon–6pm*
Open longer hours
Restaurants, bars
Tinseltown (**D** E3)
→ *44 St John St, EC1 Daily noon–4am*
American-style diner.
Bar Italia (**B** B3)
→ *22 Frith St, W1 (until 3am on Sun)*
Pizza, panini, bagels and great coffee.
Beigel Bakery (**J** A1)
→ *159 Brick Lane, E1*
An institution.
Vingt-Quatre (**G** B3)
→ *325 Fulham Rd, SW3*
A posh diner.
Pharmacy
Zafash (**G** A3)
→ *233 Old Brompton Rd, SW5; Tel. 020 7373 2798*

EATING OUT

Whether it be cutting edge or traditional, the variety of good-quality cuisine

available in London is tremendous.
Value for money
Fish & chips (white fish deep-fried in batter, with chunky chips) to eat in or take out is a substantial meal; or the UK's adopted national dish... a curry!
Pre-/post-theater menu
A reasonably priced prix fixe menu in the early (5– 6.30pm) or late (10–11pm) part of the evening.
Pubs and gastropubs
Basic meals at reasonable prices. The food is more refined and more expensive in gastropubs.
Tipping
A 12.5% charge is often automatically added to the bill. If it is, you do not need to leave a further tip.

MARKETS

Vintage clothes, bric-à-brac, second-hand
Petticoat Lane (**C** F3)

→ *Middlesex St Sun-Fri 10am–4pm*
London's oldest street market, a mix of antique and second-hand.
Brick Lane (**J** A4)
→ *Streets around Brick Lane Sun 8am–3pm*
Petticoat Lane's slightly more expensive rival.
Old Spitalfields Market
→ *see **C***
Camden Markets
→ *See **D***
Portobello Road Market
→ *See **F***
Flowers
Columbia Road Market
→ *See **J***
Food
Borough Market
→ *See **I***

GOING OUT

Nightlife
The city is famous for top-quality music of all genres. As well as famous clubs, there are numerous bars

MILLENNIUM BRIDGE AND ST PAUL'S CATHEDRAL

EAST END MARKETS

and pubs with live music.

Shows
→ ticketmaster.co.uk
→ lastminute.com

SHOPPING

Fashion
Streetwear in Soho (**B**); department stores and flagship chains on Oxford and Regent streets (**B**, **E**); luxury labels on Sloane Street; Gothic and leatherware in Camden (**D**); alternative in Shoreditch (**C**), Dover St (**A**), Columbia Road (**J**) and Brick Lane (**J**).

Food halls
Extraordinary in the world-renowned Harrods (**G** D1); also in Selfridges (**E** C4) and Fortnum and Mason (**A** B1).

Record stores
There are many second-hand record stores in Soho, Camden and Notting Hill.

SEEING LONDON

By bus
City buses
Pass by London's main monuments with nos 11 (Victoria–Liverpool St) and 15 (Marble Arch–Tower Bridge).
London Duck Tours
→ londonducktours.co.uk
This amphibious duck-shaped bus ends its journey in the Thames.
By boat
London River Service
tfl.gov.uk
Boat trips on the Thames.
MBNA Thames Clippers
→ thamesclippers.com
A hop-on, hop-off river bus linking Putney (off **G** A4) and Greenwich (**J** E4) subway stations.
On foot
London Walks
walks.com
Offers over 100 guided group walks every week; also various day trips.

SPORTS

Lord's (**E** A1)
→ St John's Wood Rd, NW8
lords.org
Cricket ground hosting the finals of the most important test matches.
Epsom Downs
→ Epsom (Surrey); train from London Waterloo station
Famous horse-racing course (hosts the Oaks and the Derby).
Twickenham Stadium
→ Whitton Road, TW2
englandrugby.com/twickenham
Six Nations rugby matches are played (Jan to March).
Wimbledon Tennis Stadium
→ Church Road, SW19
Home to one of the four Grand Slam tournaments; has a museum and tours.
Wembley Stadium
→ Wembley Park or Wembley Central subway stations
Mecca of English football.

LATEST TRENDS

Up-and-coming areas
Kings Cross (**D** D3)
The area around the train station has been transformed: terraces, food trucks and a play area with fountains on Granary Square, while an old gasometer has been turfed over to become Gasholder Park.
Peckham Rye
(off map **J** D4)
→ Peckham Rye train station
An emerging neighborhood to the south: stores and cafés on Bellenden Road and Peckham Road, and the South London Gallery, which promotes new talent: exhibitions, performance, films
southlondongallery.org
East End markets
The East End markets have experienced a revival. A feast of colors and scents at Broadway market in Hackney (off map **J** B1) (Sat 9am–5pm; London Fields train station) and Colombia Road Flower Market (**J** A3).
Pop-ups
→ londonpopups.com
Pop-up (temporary) restaurants, bars, shops, galleries and music venues set up in otherwise-unused spaces are all the rage. They can even be found in private homes.
Open-air cinema
→ rooftopfilmclub.com
In summer, rooftops in Hoxton, Stratford, Kensington and Peckham are turned into outdoor cinemas – with deckchairs (and blankets for cool nights).

CHANGING OF THE GUARD

BRITISH MUSEUM

HYDE PARK

NOTTING HILL

WESTMINSTER

 Welcome to London

R TIGER

FORTNUM & MASON

JERMYN STREET

CAFÉ, CULTURAL CENTER

Inn The Park (C2) **7**
→ St James's Park, SW1
Tel. 020 7451 9999
Daily 8am (9am Sat-Sun)–
11pm (5pm Oct-March)
Overlooking the lake at the heart of St James's Park is Oliver Peyton's stylish, curved wood-and-glass building with a large covered terrace. The perfect place to stop for breakfast, lunch or tea.

Institute of Contemporary Arts / ICA (C1) **8**
→ The Mall, Carlton House Terrace, SW1
Tel. 020 7930 3647; Café bar: Tue-Sun 11am–11pm; Galleries: Tue-Sun 11am–6pm (9pm Thu); Bookstore: Tue-Sun 11am–9pm
A haunt of Britain's avant-garde since 1948, this multicultural space – half gallery, half movie theater– shows underground films or little-known classics; also hosts lectures, club nights and exhibitions.

BARS, CLUBS

Gordon's Wine Bar (D1) **9**
→ 47 Villiers St, WC2
Mon-Sat 11am–11pm;
Sun noon–10pm
Located in the depths of an ancient cellar, there are over 100 vintages to taste in this long, candlelit room – or outside on the grass in Embankment Gardens.

Tiles (A4) **10**
→ 36 Buckingham Palace Rd, SW1
Tel. 020 7834 7761
Mon-Fri noon–3pm,
5.30–11pm
A cozy wine bar across from Victoria Station, with a warm decor and plush sofas in the basement, where the atmosphere is slightly more jazzy.

Cinnamon Club (C4) **11**
→ The Old Westminster Library, Great Smith St, SW1
Tel. 020 7222 2555
Restaurant: Mon-Fri 7.30–10am, noon–2.45pm, 6–10.45pm; Sat noon–2.45pm, 6–10.45pm. Bars: Mon-Sat 5pm (Library Bar) / 6pm (Cocktail Bar)–midnight
This striking former Victorian library building houses a modern Indian restaurant serving refined takes on classics, signatures dishes and tasting menus. The two bars – one in the old Reading Room, and the cocktail bar down the marble stairs – feature a great range of bellinis (try the cinnamon one), lassis and martinis. Bar food.

Tiger Tiger (C1) **12**
→ 29 Haymarket, SW1
Mon-Sat noon–3am;
Sun noon–midnight
With a restaurant, three bars and two dance floors, this is a vibrant and noisy spot at night but a quiet place to hang out during the day.

Heaven (D1) **13**
→ Under the arches in Villiers St, WC2
Tel. 020 7930 2020
Mon, Thu-Fri 11pm–5.30am (4am Thu-Fri);
Sat 10pm–5am
Beneath the train track at Charing Cross are drag queens, topless barmen and gogo dancers in a loud labyrinth that is popular at a gay venue.

SHOPPING

Fortnum & Mason (B1) **14**
→ 181 Piccadilly, W1
Mon-Sat 10am–8pm;
Sun 11.30am–6pm
The legendary, ornate 300-year-old food hall is full to overflowing with teas, shortbreads, marmalades, chutneys and other exquisite, expensive fare. Tearoom and restaurants.

Waterstone's (B1) **15**
→ 203-206 Piccadilly, W1
Mon-Sat 9am–10pm;
Sun 12.30–6pm
A five-story bookstore, with more than one million books in stock and comfy chairs to read them in. The fifth-floor bar/café has views of the Houses of Parliament. A few doors down is Hatchards, London's oldest bookshop (1797).

Jermyn Street (B1) **16**
This reputed street is home to fine men's tailors, shirt makers and suppliers of leather goods; also food and wine merchants.
Davidoff of London (no. 35): a quality cigar store.
Turnbull & Asser (no. 71): bespoke shirts.
Floris (no. 89): soaps, fragrances and shaving accessories since 1730.

Lock & Co (B2) **17**
→ 6 St James's St
Tel. 020 7930 8874
Founded in 1676, the most renowned hat store in town.

Lobb (B2) **18**
→ 9 St James's St
Tel. 020 7930 3664
Established in 1949, this artisan cobbler is known for its high-quality, made-to-measure footwear.

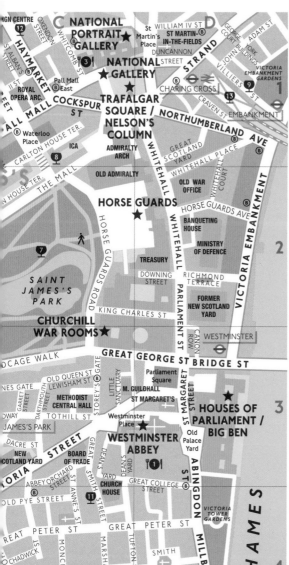

12 OXENDON STREET

C NATIONAL PORTRAIT ★ GALLERY

GN CENTRE

HAYMARKET
WHITCOMB ST
ST ALBAN'S STREET

St Martin's Place

WILLIAM IV ST
ST MARTIN- Ⓑ
IN-THE-FIELDS
DUNCANNON STREET

D GEORGE COURT
YORK
ADAM ST

JOHN BUILDINGS

STRAND

VICTORIA
EMBANKMENT
GARDENS

3 NATIONAL ★ GALLERY

Pall Mall
Ⓑ East

CHARING CROSS Ⓑ

VILLIERS ST

9 ST

1

ROYAL
OPERA ARC.

COCKSPUR ST

TRAFALGAR
SQUARE /
NELSON'S
COLUMN

CRAVEN'S EMBANKMENT

13

LL MALL

Ⓑ Waterloo
Place

CARLTON HOUSE TER.

ICA

8

CARLTON HOUSE TER.

N HOUSE TER.

THE MALL

ADMIRALTY
ARCH

OLD ADMIRALTY

/ NORTHUMBERLAND AVE Ⓑ

GREAT
SCOTLAND
YARD

WHITEHALL PLACE Ⓑ

OLD WAR
OFFICE

WHITEHALL
COURT

WHITEHALL

HORSE GUARDS ★

HORSE GUARDS AVE Ⓑ

BANQUETING
HOUSE

MINISTRY
OF DEFENCE

VICTORIA EMBANKMENT

2

7

SAINT
JAMES'S
PARK

HORSE GUARDS ROAD

TREASURY

DOWNING
STREET

RICHMOND
TERRACE

KING CHARLES ST

WHITEHALL

PARLIAMENT ST

FORMER
NEW SCOTLAND
YARD

CANON
ROW

WESTMINSTER

CHURCHILL
WAR ROOMS ★

DCAGE WALK

GREAT GEORGE ST

BRIDGE ST

NES GATE
OLD QUEEN ST
LEWISHAM ST

GARRET
STREET
DARTMOUTH
ST

METHODIST
CENTRAL HALL

TOTHILL ST

JAMES'S PARK

DACRE ST

NEW
COTLAND YARD

TORIA

STOREY'S Ⓑ GATE

LITTLE
SANCTUARY

Parliament
Square

M. GUILDHALL
ST MARGARET'S

Westminster
Place

BOARD
OF TRADE

STREET

OLD PYE STREET

ABBEY ORCHARD
STREET

Ⓑ

DEAN'S
YARD

DEAN'S
YARD

ST ANNE'S ST

CHURCH
HOUSE

11

WESTMINSTER
ABBEY ★ **1**

Old
Palace
Yard

GREAT COLLEGE
STREET

PARLIAMENT
STREET

ST MARGARET
STREET

★
HOUSES OF
PARLIAMENT /
BIG BEN

3

ABINGDON ST Ⓑ

VICTORIA
TOWER
GARDENS

REAT
PETER ST

CHADWICK

MEDWAY STRE

GREAT PETER ST

JS ST

MONCK STRE

MARSHAM ST

TUFTON STREET

SMITH

SQUARE

BRP
ST

MILLBANK

THAMES

4

T H A M E S

BUCKINGHAM PALACE / R. MEWS

"LET US
GO FORWARD
TOGETHER"

CHURCHILL WAR ROOMS

HOUSES OF PARLIAMENT /
BIG BEN

There is never a quiet moment in the area between Oxford Circus and Covent Garden. By day the mood is set by the bustling shoppers along Regent Street and Oxford Street, and by hungry tourists strolling through Chinatown or sitting at the café-terraces of Covent Garden. In the evening, devotees of plays and musicals descend on the theaters; and cosmopolitan Soho's many restaurants, gay bars and sex shops draw teeming crowds. Further north, Bloomsbury, with its rich literary heritage, represents learning, with the British Museum and UCL (University College London) as its emblems.

SPUNTINO

YAUATCHA

RESTAURANTS

Chinatown (B4-C4)
The Chinese quarter abounds with restaurants:
Bao (B4) ❶
→ 53 Lexington Street, W1
Mon-Sat noon–3pm,
5.30–10pm
A *bao* is a Taiwanese steamed bun filled with braised pork and sprinkled with peanuts. Its popularity is evident by the line of people outside this restaurant.
New World (C4) ❷
→ 1 Gerrard Place, W1
Tel. 020 7734 0677
Daily 11am–midnight
Dim-sum and other Cantonese specialties.
Polpetto (B3) ❸
→ 11 Berwick St, W1
Tel. 020 7439 8627; Daily noon–11am (10.30pm Sun)
Small Venetian dishes combined to create a whole meal: fried zucchini, risotto balls, octopus in its ink, osso bucco. Entrées £5–8.
Spuntino (B4) ❹
→ 61 Rupert St, W1; no tel.
Daily noon–midnight
(1am Thu-Sat, 11pm Sun)
Bringing a taste of Brooklyn to Soho, the menu is made of small sharing plates: truffled egg toast, eggplant fries, and a twist on the

peanut-and-jelly sandwich and the signature sliders (mini-burgers). £5–10.
10 Greek St (C3) ❺
→ 10 Greek St, W1
Tel. 020 7734 4677
Mon-Sat noon–10.45pm
The streamlined decor echoes the subtle modern cuisine: sweet-potato soup with yoghurt; scallops with parsnip purée; chocolate, pear and pecan pie. Tapas available all day.
Entrées £8–20.
Andrew Edmunds (B4) ❻
→ 46 Lexington Street, W1
Tel. 020 7437 5708
Mon-Sat noon–3.30pm,
5.30–10.45pm; Sun 1–4pm,
6–10.30pm
A delightful 18th-century house with a bar and a few tables in the small dining room. The menu includes roast quail with garlic mayonnaise, marrowbone with sweet onions, scallops with spicy *sobrasada* sausage.
Entrées £12–20.
Yauatcha (B3) ❼
→ 15-17 Broadwick St, W1
Tel. 020 7494 8888
Daily noon–10pm
(10.30pm Fri-Sat)
Very good quality, contemporary Chinese dining with expertly

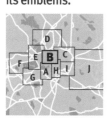

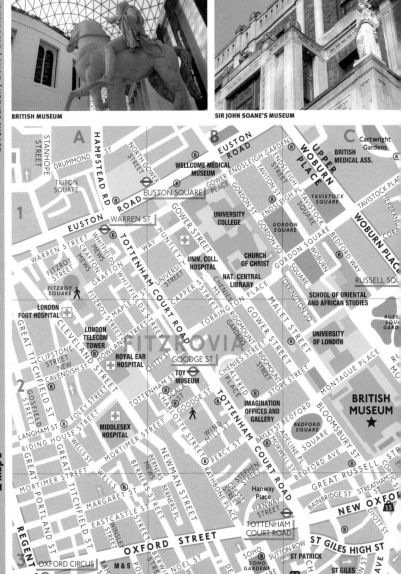

LONDON TRANSPORT MUSEUM

COVENT GARDEN

★ **British Museum** (C2)
→ *Great Russell St, WC1*
Daily 10am–5.30pm
(8.30pm Fri)
In 1753, Dr Hans Sloane bequeathed his collection of curios to the nation. This formed the nucleus of the museum, which now has one of the world's greatest collections of antiquities and ethnographic works, including the Rosetta Stone and the Parthenon frieze. The interior courtyard (the Great Court) is covered with a huge steel and glass ceiling (Norman Foster, 2000). Don't miss the magnificent domed Reading Room.

★ **Sir John Soane's Museum** (E3)
→ *13 Lincoln's Inn Fields, WC2*
Tel. 020 7405 2107; Tue-Sat 10am–5.30pm (visits by candle light on the first Tue of every month, 6–9pm; arrive early
Sir John Soane (1753–1837), a renowned architect, art lover and eccentric turned his home into a remarkable museum housing a collection of antiquities, books and paintings by Hogarth, Watteau, etc.

★ **Dr Johnson's House** (F3)
→ *17 Gough Square*
Tel. 020 7353 3745; Mon-Sat 11am–5.30pm (5pm Oct-April)
Behind the 17th-century

red brick façade of this house, the lexicographer Samuel Johnson (1709–84) lived and worked for nine years compiling his famous dictionary of the English language (1755); furniture, manuscripts, memorabilia.

★ **Temple** (F4)
This district, owned by the Knights Templar from 1185–1312, is like a small enclave within the city. Two of the four Law Schools took up residence here in the 17th century. Around Middle Temple Lane is a labyrinth of streets, small courtyards and private gardens. This is also the site of the famous Middle Temple Hall, where

Shakespeare's comedy *Twelfth Night* was premie in 1600.

★ **Somerset House** (
→ *Strand, WC2; Tel. 020 7 4600; Daily 10am–6pm*
William Chambers' supe neoclassical palace (17 with fountains playing i courtyard, contains a precious art collection bequeathed to the natio and an exhibition space
Courtauld Gallery (E4)
The collection of the industrialist Samuel Courtauld (1876–1947), enhanced by other donations, is best know for its Impressionist and Postimpressionist pictu

B

WESTMINSTER ABBEY

TATE BRITAIN

Map labels:
ROAD · HORSEFERRY RD · LAMBETH BRIDGE · PAGE STREET · ST JOHN'S GARDENS · THORNEY ST · MILLBANK · MILLBANK TOWER · VINCENT STREET · RIVER · 5 · TATE BRITAIN · WESTMINSTER · VAUXHALL BRIDGE ROAD · PIMLICO · ATTERBURY ST · PONSONBY PL. · PONSONBY TER. · BESSBOROUGH ST · BESSBOROUGH GARDENS · LINDSAY SQUARE · BESSBOROUGH PLACE · GROSVENOR ROAD · VAUXHALL BRIDGE · ALBERT EMBANKMENT · 6 · VAUXHALL · ST GEORGE WHARF · VAUXHALL

...rds draws crowds all
r. Look out for a raised
: it means the Queen
. residence. Also
the Royal Mews'
gnificent collection of
monial stage coaches
. carriages.

Queen's Gallery (A3)
→ *uckingham Gate, SW1*
020 7766 7301; Daily 10am
oam July-Sep)–5.30pm
. neoclassical-style
ery, on the west front
.uckingham Palace, was
.uilt in 1962 out of the
.nb-damaged ruins of
.former private chapel.
.splays a changing
.ction from the Royal
.ection's 9,000 artworks

– one of the richest private
collections in the world.
**★ Churchill War
Rooms** (C3)
→ *Clive Steps, King Charles St,
SW1; Tel. 020 7930 6961
Daily 9.30am–6pm*
These reinforced chambers
played a crucial role in
history as Churchill's HQ
during World War Two.
Faithful reconstruction of
life in the underground
complex, and an
interactive 50-ft long
lifeline of Churchill's life.
**★ Houses of
Parliament/
Big Ben** (D3)
→ *Margaret St, SW1
Tel. 020 7219 4114; Guided*

*tours daily 9am–4.15pm
(every 15–20 mins); reserve*
The 13-ton bell known as
Big Ben chimes the hours
and quarters. The neo-
Gothic architecture of the
houses was designed by
Charles Barry and Augustus
Pugin after fire destroyed
the previous building in
1834. You can sit in on
debates when the Houses
are sitting (meeting).
**★ Westminster
Abbey** (D3)
→ *Dean's Yard, SW1
Tel. 020 7222 5152; Mon-Sat
9.30am–3.30pm (1.30pm Sat)*
The finest religious building
in London, a masterpiece
of flamboyant Gothic.

Coronations have taken
place here beneath the high
ribbed vaulting since 1308
(the actual Coronation
Chair used in the ceremony
is on view in one of the
chapels). Many famous
people are buried in the
Abbey – the most famous
tomb is that of King Edward
the Confessor (1042–66).
★ Tate Britain (D5)
→ *Millbank, SW1
Daily 10am–6pm*
English art from 1500 to
the present day – Hogarth,
Gainsborough, Reynolds,
the Pre-Raphaelites. The
adjacent Clore Gallery
houses the marvelous
Turner collection.

Business people fill the streets here during the week, but on weekends the City is like a ghost town. Relics of the past, spared by the Great Fire of 1666 and thebombs of World War Two, offer a glimpse into the historic heart of London. The maze of streets and passages hold some surprises as granite and concrete 1970s office blocks stand alongside old pubs, historic churches and 21st-century glass-and-steel skyscrapers. To the north east, not far from Spitalfields market, young artists and creators of all kinds give Shoreditch and Hoxton a bohemian feel, while Clerkenwell, to the north west, draws media types and designers.

PIZZA EAST

ST JOHN BREAD & WINE

RESTAURANTS

Viet Grill (E1) 🍴❶
→ 58 Kingsland Rd, EC2
Tel. 020 7739 6686
Daily 11am–11pm (11.30pm Fri-Sat, 10.30pm Sun)
Fine Vietnamese street food. Great pho (noodle soup with a rich beef broth). Entrées £8–12.

Busaba Eathai (E1) 🍴❷
→ 319 Old St, EC1
Tel. 020 7729 0808
Daily noon–11pm (11.30pm Fri-Sat, 10.30pm Sun)
Fresh and subtle flavors in this Thai eatery where the decor is all wood and clean lines. Entrées £8–13.

8 Hoxton Square (E1) 🍴❸
→ 8 Hoxton Square
Tel. 020 7729 4232; Mon-Fri noon–11pm; Sat-Sun 10am–11pm (5pm Sun)
This restaurant's British-Italian fusion is thriving in the midst of a newly fashionable area: confit of pork with red cabbage and chestnuts; pumpkin-burrata pie; chocolate terrine and poached pear with honey. £8–16.

Pizza East (E2) 🍴❹
→ 56 Shoreditch High St
Tel. 020 7729 1888
Mon-Fri noon–11pm (midnight Thu, 1am Fri); Sat-Sun 10am–1am (11pm Sun)
An industrial look to this pizza restaurant where diners share long tables. Entrées £9–17.

The Peasant (B1) 🍴❺
→ 240 St John St, EC1
Tel. 020 7336 7726
Restaurant: Tue-Sat 6–10.30pm; Pub: daily noon–11pm (10.30pm Sun)
This atmospheric Victorian pub has a beautiful curved horseshoe counter and a restaurant upstairs serving a European menu: stilton fritters with walnuts and grape chutney; braised ox cheek with parsnip mashed potato; pear and blackberry crumble. Entrées £10–15 (pub); £20–24 (restaurant).

Tramshed (E1) 🍴❻
→ 32 Rivington St, EC2
Tel. 020 7749 0478
Daily 11am–11pm (midnight Sat, 9.30pm Sun)
A fashionable restaurant, as suggested by the work of contemporary artist Damien Hirst that dominates the dining room. The menu is based on poultry and steak. Entrées £14–45.

St John Bread & Wine (F2) 🍴❼
→ 94-96 Commercial St, E1

MONUMENT

ST STEPHEN WALBROOK

LEADENHALL MARKET

▲ Map B

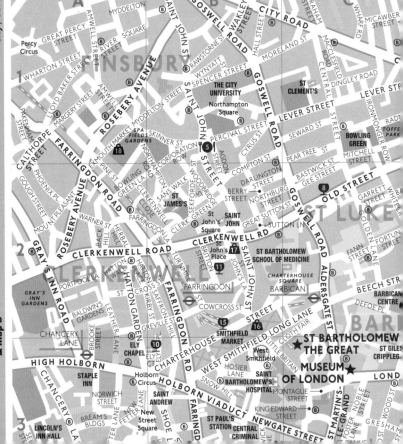

MB & FLAG

NEAL STREET

LIBERTY

crafted dim-sum and handmade sweets and pastries. Sleek decor. Entrées £14–26.

TEAROOMS, ICE-CREAM PARLOR

Gelupo (B4) **8**
→ 7 Archer St, W1
Tel. 020 7287 5555; Mon-Fri 11am–11pm (midnight Fri); Sun noon–11pm
Jacob Kenedy and Victor Hugo opened this gelateria-deli across from their trattoria Bocca di Lupo (recommended). The granitas, sorbets and gelati are heavenly, with flavors changing according to the season.

Princi (B3) **9**
→ 135 Wardour St, W1
Mon-Sat 8am–midnight; Sun 8.30am–10pm
This London outpost of the chic Milanese bakery from Rocco Princi has appetizing focaccia, pizza, pastries and bread baked on site. Leave room for a cupcake from Hummingbird's Bakery, at no. 155.

Maison Bertaux (C3) **10**
→ 28 Greek St, W1
Tel. 020 7437 6007
Mon-Sat 8.30am–11pm; Sun 9.30am–8pm
London's oldest (1871)

patisserie and tea rooms, with marble-topped tables, plus art gallery spaces.

MOVIE THEATER, PUB, MUSIC VENUES

Lamb & Flag (C4) **11**
→ 33 Rose St, WC2
Mon-Sat 11am–11pm; Sun noon–10.30pm
The oldest pub in Covent Garden (1623). Very popular, with a wide choice of whiskies.

Picturehouse Central (B4) **12**
→ Corner of Great Windmill St and Shaftesbury Ave
Tel. 0871 5902 5755
Originally built as an elegant restaurant in 1896, the Trocadero now contains a comfortable 7-screen multiplex that screens blockbusters (sometimes in 3D), as well as independent films. Bar-restaurant.

Ronnie Scott's (B3) **13**
47 Frith St, W1; Tel. 020 7439 0747; Mon-Sat 6pm–1am (3am Fri-Sat); Sun noon–4pm, 6.30pm–midnight
Stars such as Sonny Rollins and Nina Simone have graced the stage of this legendary jazz club since the 1960s. The

program is more eclectic nowadays, taking in flamenco and DJ sets.

The Borderline (C3) **14**
→ Orange Yard, Manette St, W1; Tel. 020 7734 5547
Wed-Sat 7pm–4am (3am Wed); open outside of these times if concerts are planned
Intimate music space showcasing blues, rock and alternative bands. Also club nights.

SHOPPING

James Smith & Sons (C3) **15**
→ 53 New Oxford St, WC2
Tel. 020 7836 4731
Mon-Sat 10am (10.30am Wed)–5.45pm (5.15pm Sat)
Behind an ornate Victorian façade Smith & Sons has been selling and repairing walking-sticks and umbrellas since 1830.

Neal Street (C3-D3) **16**
Lively street with an assortment of fashion and shoe stores.

Liberty (A3) **17**
→ Great Marlborough St, W1; Mon-Sat 10am–8pm; Sun noon–6pm
Begun in the 19th century as an outlet for the Arts and Crafts movement, the famous 'Tudor House' remains a

leading stockist of designer items.

Burlington Arcade (A4) **18**
→ 51 Piccadilly, W1
Mon-Sat 9am–7.30pm; Sun 11am–6pm
Famous covered shopping arcade uniting Piccadilly and Bond St. Elegant stores: jewelry, cashmere items, perfumes, accessories.

Hamleys (A4) **19**
→ 188-196 Regent St, W1
Mon-Fri 10am–8pm (9pm Thu-Fri); Sat 9.30am–9pm; Sun noon–6pm
Thousands of games and toys over seven floors.

Carnaby Street / Kingly Court (A3-A4) **20**
Once the symbol of the swinging 1960s, now an altogether more modern affair. Don't miss Kingly Court, a pretty three-story galleried courtyard with some interesting shops.

Soho's specialist record stores (B3) **21**
Indie (**Sister Ray** at no. 34 Berwickß St); second-hand (**Reckless Records** at no. 30 Berwick St); dance and electro (**Phonica Records** at no. 51 Poland St); New Wave, reggae, electro (**Sounds of the Universe** at 7 Broadwick St).

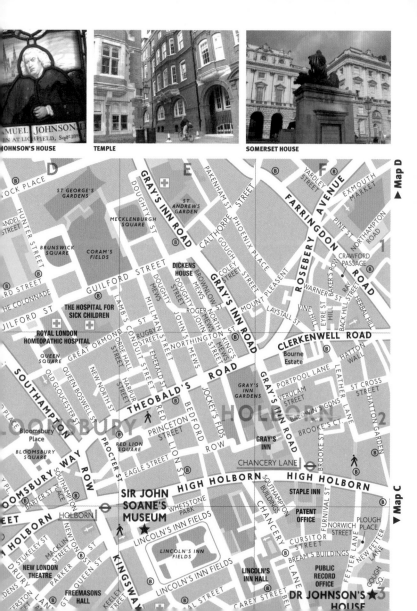

JOHNSON'S HOUSE

TEMPLE

SOMERSET HOUSE

▲ Map D

▼ Map C

Map labels: ROYAL OPERA HOUSE, ST PHILIP'S HOSP., ROYAL COURTS OF JUSTICE, FLEET STREET, DRURY LANE, ACRE STREET, KEMBLE STREET, KEAN ST, CLEMENTS INN PASS, ST CLEMENT DANES, STRAND, TEMPLE CHURCH, TUDOR STREET, DRURY LANE THEATRE, ALDWYCH, BUSH HOUSE, STRAND, ESSEX ST, MIDDLE TEMPLE LANE, TEMPLE, INNER TEMPLE GARDEN, TEMPLE AVENUE, COVENT GARDEN, THEATRE MUSEUM, RUSSELL STREET, BOW STREET, CATHERINE ST, COURTAULD GALLERY, SURREY STREET, ARUNDEL ST, MILFORD LANE, MIDDLE TEMPLE GARDEN, COVENT GARDEN, LYCEUM THEATRE, LONDON TRANSPORT MUSEUM, SOMERSET HOUSE, TEMPLE, TEMPLE PLACE, Covent Garden Piazza, PAUL'S CHURCH, HENRIETTA STREET, MAIDEN LANE, STRAND, LANCASTER PLACE, EMBANKMENT GALLERY, VICTORIA EMBANKMENT, SAVOY, JOHN ADAM ST, SAVOY PL, VICTORIA EMBANKMENT, WATERLOO BRIDGE, RIVER THAMES, 0 100 200 m, RTIN-FIELDS, D, E, F, 4

AL OPERA HOUSE

ROYAL ACADEMY OF ARTS

uch artists as Pissarro,
anne, Monet, Renoir,
guin, Van Gogh and
digliani. There is also
nity by Botticelli, 32
ks by Rubens, several
paintings by Turner
gouaches by Rouault.

bankment Gallery E4
ign, contemporary art,
hitecture and fashion in
rooms which formerly
used the Gilbert
ection (now in the
Museum, **G** C2)

London Transport
Museum (D4)
Covent Garden Piazza, WC2
ly 10am (11am Fri)–6pm
ated in one of Covent
den's former floral halls

(1871), this museum has
vehicles, posters, signs,
uniforms and photos dating
back to the 18th century.

★ **Royal Opera**
House (D3)
→ *Tel. 020 7304 4000; Tours*
(1hr 15 mins) by reservation:
Mon-Sat 10.30am–2.30pm
The most prestigious opera
house in the city. Upgrade
works (due for completion
at the end of 2017) will
include new entrances on
Bow Street and the Covent
Garden Piazza and an
enlarged main foyer.

★ **Covent Garden** (D4)
Once the vegetable garden
of the convent attached to
Westminster Abbey and

the site of an early fruit
and vegetable market. The
square, designed by Inigo
Jones (1631), remains very
popular – the pretty arched
gallery (1832) and the iron
and glass market halls
house stores, craft stalls,
cafés, restaurants and
street entertainers.

★ **St Martin-in-**
the-Fields (C4)
→ *Trafalgar Square, WC2*
Tel. 020 7766 1100
Mon-Fri 8.30am–1pm,
2–6pm (5pm Wed); Sat
9.30am–6pm; Sun 3.30–5pm
Designed by James Gibb
in 1726, it transformed
the architectural style of
English religious buildings.

Free lunchtime concerts
(1pm Mon, Tue, Fri) and
candlelit music evenings.

★ **Royal Academy**
of Arts (A4)
→ *Burlington House, W1*
Tel. 020 7300 8000; Daily
10am–6pm (10pm Fri); Tours
(1 hr) of the John Madejski
Fine Rooms: Tue 1pm; Wed-Fri
1pm, 3pm; Sat 11.30am
The Summer Exhibition
here still draws the crowds,
as do the big-name shows
that run through the year.
The John Madejski Fine
Rooms include works by
British painters such as
Gainsborough, Reynolds,
Turner, Stanley Spencer
and David Hockney.

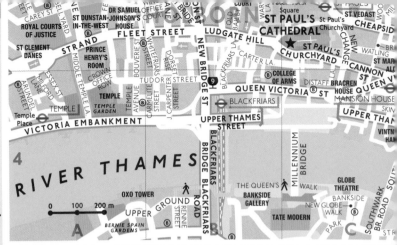

GUILDHALL

ST PAUL'S CATHEDRAL

MUSEUM OF LONDON

★ **Monument** (D4)
→ Monument St, EC3
Tel. 020 7626 2717
Daily 9.30am–6pm
Erected to commemorate the Great Fire (1666), this impressive 200-ft-tall column conceals a marble staircase (311 steps) leading to the top.

★ **St Stephen Walbrook** (D4)
→ 39 Walbrook St, EC4
Tel. 020 7626 9000; Mon-Fri 10am–3.30pm (3pm Wed)
Completed in 1680, this is one of Christopher Wren's most elaborate and classical designs. The dome is based on Wren's original design for St Paul's.

★ **20 Fenchurch Street** (E4)
→ 20 Fenchurch St, EC3
Mon-Fri 10am–6pm; Sat-Sun 11am–9pm. Access without reservation: 10–11.30am, 2–4.30pm
In 2014, when Rafael Viñoly's 'Walkie-Talkie' skyscraper was completed, it was found that the building's round windows bounced back sunlight and scorched the bodywork of vehicles below. Thus, protective awnings had to be installed. The 35th floor offers a 360-degree view from the Sky Garden bar and open-air terrace (visits of up to 1 hr), as well as a

sophisticated restaurant.

★ **Leadenhall Market** (E3)
→ Gracechurch St, EC3
Market (jewelry, objets d'art, flowers): Mon-Fri 10am–6pm
An opulent Victorian market hall with metal arches surmounted by a glass dome at the intersection of its aisles. Above it loom the six aluminium towers of the Lloyd's Building complex (Richard Rogers, 1986).

★ **Swiss Re Tower** (E3)
→ 30 St Mary Axe, EC3
Architect Norman Foster's distinctive work (2004) named after the Swiss Re Company which

commissioned it. The 41-story, 591-ft-high to is covered with blue ar black glass lozenges a its unusual bullet shap has earned it the nickn of The Gherkin.

★ **Bank of England Museum** (D3)
→ Bartholomew Lane, EC
Tel. 020 7601 5545
Mon-Fri 10am–5pm
The history and day-to running of the 'Old Lac Threadneedle Street', powerful Bank of Engla founded in 1694, whic stores the nation's gol Exhibits include bankn – real and counterfeit – gold ingots, etc.

BLACK FRIAR

CARGO

A. GOLD

Tel. 020 7251 0848; Daily 9am–11pm (9pm Mon); Breakfast: daily 9am–noon
Those interested in contemporary eating – and in offal in particular – will know Fergus Henderson's St John (26 St John St, **C** B2). This more informal spot offers a simpler version of the same classics: crispy pig's cheek with dandelion and shallots; roast beef and bone marrow mash. Delicious homemade bread and desserts. Entrées £15–20.

CAFÉ, PUBS, CULTURAL CENTER

Look Mum No Hands (C2) 🔟⑧
→ 49 Old St, EC1
Tel. 020 7253 1025
Daily 7.30am (8.30am Sat, 9.30am Sun)–10pm
The founders of this café (with a bicycle workshop at the back) wanted to merge their love of cycling with their passion for coffee and fresh, seasonal food. Salads, pies, homemade cakes and good coffee.

The Black Friar (B4) ⑨
→ 174 Queen Victoria St, EC4; Mon-Sat 10am–11pm; Sun noon–8.30pm

Mosaics, polychrome marble and carved monks of all sizes decorate this fantastic Arts and Crafts (1905) pub, famous for its extravagant decor.

Ye Old Mitre (B3) 🔟
→ 1 Ely Court, via 8 Hatton Garden, EC1
Mon-Fri 11am–11pm
Down a hidden alleyway is this oak-fronted pub, one of London's oldest (1546), where city workers flock after work.

The Jerusalem Tavern (B2) ⑪
→ 55 Britton St, EC1
Mon-Fri 11am–11pm
Another pub of great charm with excellent beers, including a surprising one with honey, and a ruby red ale.

Barbican Centre (C2) ⑫
→ Silk St, EC2
Tel. 020 7638 4141
Daily 9am (noon Sun)–11pm
barbican.org.uk
The home of the London Symphony Orchestra is also a multidisciplinary art center: music, theater, dance, cinema, visual art.

MUSIC VENUE, BAR, CLUBS

Dream Bags JaguarShoes (E1) ⑬
→ 32-34 Kingsland Rd

Tel. 020 7683 0912
Daily noon–1am
Hip café-bar-gallery space hosting music events, lectures, workshops, fashion shows and Sunday markets and art fairs.

Cargo (E1) ⑭
→ 83 Rivington St, EC2
Daily noon–1am (3am Fri-Sat, midnight Sun)
Atmospheric venue for bands and big-name DJs in a disused railway yard.

Fabric (B2) ⑮
→ 77a Charterhouse St, EC1
fabriclondon.com
This legendary club welcomes the best DJs in the world and the most knowledgeable of dance-music-loving crowds.

SHOPPING

Smithfield Market (B2) ⑯
→ Charterhouse St, EC1
Mon-Fri 3am–9am (arrive before 7am)
Since 1868 the monumental Victorian buildings designed by Sir Horace Jones, with beautiful cast-iron arches, glass-roofed halls and red-brick walls have housed a meat market.

Craft Central (B2) ⑰
→ 33-35 St John's Square, EC1; Mon-Sat 10am–7pm

A space dedicated to the promotion of fine craft and design skills, with over 100 designer-maker's creations to browse.

Exmouth Market (A1) ⑱
A pedestrianized street with a flock of independent boutiques, cafés and restaurants. The market (Fri-Sat) is home to enticing street-food stands.

Old Spitalfields Market (F2) ⑲
→ 16 Horner Square, E1
Daily 10am (11am Sat)–5pm
There has been a covered market on this site since 1682 and people still flock here to seek out artisan crafts, jewelry, clothes and organic products. Thursdays are dedicated to antiques and vintage. The area around the market is worth exploring, too.

A. Gold (F2) ⑳
→ 42 Brushfield St, E1
Mon-Fri 10am–4pm; Sat-Sun noon–5pm
A village shop in the City. British produce made to traditional methods: jams, cakes, honey, chutneys, cheeses, pickles; also sandwiches with the finest fillings.

SWISS RE TOWER

BANK OF ENGLAND MUSEUM

ST BARTHOLOMEW THE GREAT

GEFFRYE MUSEUM

Guildhall (D3)
→ Gresham St, EC2
Tel. 020 7332 3700
Mon-Sat 10am–4.30pm
The heart of the City's
municipal power beats
behind this 18th-century
façade, a fusion of
Gothic, Greek and Indian
influences. The Great Hall
is decorated with the arms
of the guilds that have
elected the Lord Mayor
since 1319. The site holds
the remains of the city's
only Roman amphitheater.

**★ Museum of
London** (C3)
→ 150 London Wall, EC2
Tel. 020 7001 9844
Daily 10am–6pm

A fascinating museum
devoted to the story of
London and the life of its
people, from prehistory
to the present day, with
animated reconstructions
models, everyday items,
relics and costumes.

**★ St Paul's
Cathedral** (C3)
→ St Paul's Churchyard, EC4
Tel. 020 7246 8348
Mon-Sat 8.30am–4pm
After World War Two, Wren's
masterpiece was left intact
in the midst of the ruined
City and became the
symbol of Londoners'
spirit. The 361-ft-high
dome, completed in 1711,
is the largest in the world

after that of St Peter's in
Rome. See the superb
18th-century treasures
inside: frescoes by
Thornhill telling the story
of Saint Paul, wrought-iron
choir gates by Jean Tijou
and choir stalls by Gibbons.
The crypt holds the tombs
of Wren and Nelson.

**★ St Bartholomew
the Great** (C3)
→ Church House, Cloth Fair,
EC1; Tel. 020 7600 0440; Mon-
Fri 8.30am–5pm; Sat 10am–
4pm; Sun 8.30am–8pm
The oldest church in
London (12th c.). After
Henry VIII's ban on
religious orders (16th c.),
the north transept was

used as a forge, the crypt
as a cellar, the Lady Chapel
as a printing house and
the cloister as a stable.
The church was restored
and again used for worship
in the 19th century. The
pillars of the ambulatory
are one of the few
examples of Norman
architecture in London.

★ Geffrye Museum (E1)
→ 136 Kingsland Rd, E2
Tel. 020 7739 9893; Tue-Sun
10am–5pm. Gardens: April-Oct
A fascinating look at the
lives of the British middle
classes, with superb
reconstructions of homes
and gardens from the 17th
century to the present day.

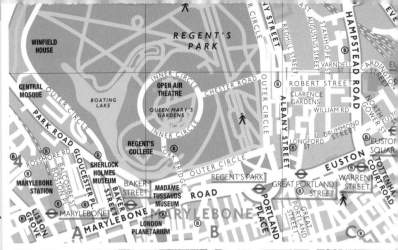

REGENT'S CANAL

ESTORICK COLLECTION

CAMDEN TOWN

★ Charles Dickens Museum (E4)
→ *48 Doughty St, WC1*
Tel. 020 7405 2127
Tue-Sun 10am–5pm
The ticking of a clock is the only sound in this narrow house where the great novelist Dickens (1812–70) lived from 1837 to 1839. Portraits and memorabilia, with a Victorian drawing room upstairs.

★ Foundling Museum (E4)
→ *40 Brunswick Square, WC1*
Tel. 020 7841 3600; Tue-Sun 10am (11am Sun)–5pm
A museum devoted to the life and work of Thomas Coram (1668–1751), who in 1739 opened the first institution for abandoned children in London. A poignant exhibition describes the misery of life on the streets contrasted with life in the refuge using engravings by Hogarth, photos and objects. Upstairs are 18th-century works by philanthropic artists (Ramsay, Reynolds), memorabilia relating to George Frideric Handel, and the stunning rococo Court Room.

★ Petrie Museum of Egyptian Archaeology (D4)
→ *Malet Place, UCL campus, WC1; Tel. 020 7679 2884*
Tue-Sat 1–5pm
On display under the strip-lighting of a university building is the collection of the Egyptologist William Flinders Petrie (1853–1942): jewelry, statuettes, stelae, amphorae, and a linen tunic dating from 2800 BC.

★ British Library (D3)
→ *96 Euston Rd, NW1*
Mon-Sat 9.30am–8pm (6pm Mon, Fri; 5pm Sat); Sun 11am–5pm
The pure lines of the current library building are the work of Colin St John Wilson (1922–2007). With 14 floors totalling 190,000 sq. ft of floor space, it contains a collection begun in the 18th century and considered to be one of the greatest in the world. Among the treasures that can be examined with the help of tactile screens or listening devices are an illuminated 15th-century Gutenberg Bible, one of Da Vinci's notebooks, manuscripts by Jane Austen and Lewis Carroll, and the famous Magna Carta, a charter of baronial rights signed by King John in 1215 beside the Thames at Runnymede.

★ London Canal Museum (E3)
→ *12-13 New Wharf Rd, N1*
Tel. 020 7713 0836

D

CHARLES DICKENS MUSEUM

FOUNDLING MUSEUM

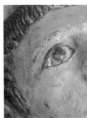

PETRIE MUSEUM OF EGYPTIAN

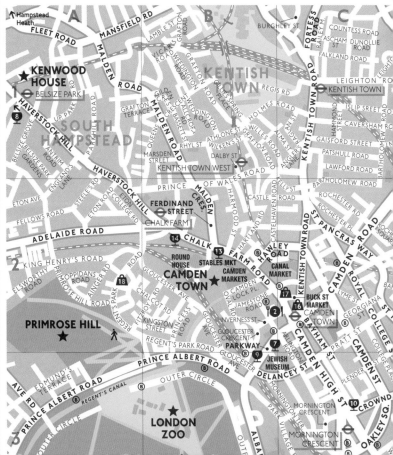

D The north London that Dickens so vividly described is no more: to the east, bars and boutiques line fashionable Upper Street in Islington. Further south is the spectacular British Library and St Pancras Station, with the area around King's Cross continuing to evolve with the development of Granary Square as a new area for cultural events, galleries and open public spaces. North-west are the markets and music spots of Camden Town, but to escape the crowds follow the canal to London Zoo, toward the picturesque green space – Primrose Hill; or to charming Hampstead Village and a walk on the Heath.

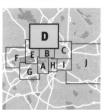

CARAVAN

NORTH SEA FISH

RESTAURANTS

Dishoom (D3)
→ 5 Stable St, N1
Mon-Fri 8am–11pm
(midnight Thu-Fri); Sat-Sun
9am–midnight (11pm Sun)
One of London's best Indian restaurants, with a checkered floor inspired by the elegant cafés of Bombay. It is set inside the Granary Building, one of the warehouses that have been refurbished in the King's Cross area. Aromatic cooking with a modern touch, including spicy omelets for breakfast. Entrées £8–12.

Haché (B2) |2|
→ 24 Inverness St, NW1
Tel. 020 7485 9100
Daily noon–10.30pm
(11pm Fri-Sat, 10pm Sun)
A family business whose venison, lamb, beef, fish and veggie burgers are repeatedly voted 'best in London' by the clientele; good fries. Burger £7–13.

Trullo (F1) |3|
→ 300-302 St Paul's Rd, N1
Tel. 020 7226 2733
Mon-Sat 12.30–2.45pm,
6–10.15pm; Sun 12.30–3pm
Confidently unfussy Italian-inspired cooking in a stylish interior of stripped wooden floors and white tablecloths. Prized for its fresh, handmade pasta and fish and meat dishes cooked over burning coals. Entrées £9–19.

Camino (E3) |4|
→ 3 Varnishers Yard,
The Regent's Quarter, N1
Tel. 020 7841 7331; Mon-Fri
noon–3pm, 6–11pm; Sat
noon–3.30pm, 5.30–11pm;
Sun 11am–3.30pm, 6–10pm
Stop at this bar/restaurant behind King's Cross station for great tapas and a glass of Andalusian sherry. Live music Thu-Sat. Entrées £9–22.50; tapas £3–12.50.

North Sea Fish (D4) |5|
→ 7-8 Leigh St, WC1
Tel. 020 7387 5892
Mon-Sat noon–2.30pm,
5.30–10.30pm
Fresh fish options include Scottish salmon, undyed smoked haddock and homemade fishcakes served with mushy peas. Takeout available. Entrées £12–20.

Caravan (D3) |6|
→ 1 Granary Square, EC1
Tel. 020 7101 7661
Mon-Fri 8am–10.30pm
(11pm Wed-Thu, midnight Fri); Sat-Sun 10am–midnight (4pm Sun)
A lively restaurant in a converted warehouse with a menu that draws

HOLLY BUSH

BRITISH BOOT COMPANY

CAMDEN MARKETS

on several culinary traditions: gnocchi with artichoke cream, trout with purée of nori seaweed. Entrées £14–22; appetizers £5–9.

TEAROOM, PUB

Yumchaa (B2) ⑦
→ 35-37 Parkway, NW1
Mon-Fri 9am–6pm;
Sat-Sun 8.30am–7pm
Housed in the former, characterful Palmers Pet Shop, over 30 different blends of tea and a selection of cakes.

The Holly Bush
(off map A1) ⑧
→ 22 Holly Mount, NW3
Daily noon–11pm
(10.30pm Sun)
A traditional pub set in a fine 17th-century building in an alley on the heights of Hampstead.

MUSIC VENUES

Dublin Castle (B3) ⑨
→ 94 Parkway, NW1
Mon-Wed 1pm–1am;
Thu-Sun noon–2am
A local legend since Madness played its first gig here in the 1970s, this pub hosts live music every night.
KOKO (C3) ⑩
→ 1a Camden High St, NW1
Tel. 020 7388 3222

Sun-Fri 7–11pm (4am Fri);
Sat 10pm–4am
This beautifully restored theater (1900) with its purple rococo interior is now a live music/club venue.
Union Chapel (F2) ⑪
→ Compton Terrace, N1
Tel. 020 7226 1686
unionchapel.org.uk
A working church that puts on concerts under its neogothic arches: folk, jazz, world music.

CULTURAL CENTERS

Kings Place (E3) ⑫
→ 90 York Way, N1
Tel. 020 7520 1490
kingsplace.co.uk
Behind a façade of undulating glass is this hub for music and art, with two auditoriums (jazz, classic and folk concerts) and two art galleries. It also houses the offices of the daily newspaper The Guardian.
Proud Camden (B2) ⑬
→ Stables Market, NW1
Wed-Sat 11am–2.30am
(1.30am Wed); Gallery:
daily 11am–5.30pm
This vast space within a 200-year-old former horses' hospital serves today as a photographic art gallery, a bar and club with live acts and DJs.

The Round House (B2) ⑭
→ Chalk Farm Rd, NW1
Tel. 020 7424 9991
This refurbished locomotive shed (1846) was the setting for concerts by Jimi Hendrix, Pink Floyd and other rock legends in the 1960s. Now it hosts an eclectic mix of live music of all kinds, as well as theater, dance, circus and cabaret.

SHOPPING

Camden Passage (F3) ⑮
→ Daily 10am–6pm
Antiques: Wed-Sun
At its best on one of its antique days, with great open-air displays of items. Bookstalls, jewelry kiosks and vintage clothes at other times.
British Boot Company (C2) ⑯
→ 5 Kentish Town Rd, NW1
Tel. 020 7485 8505
Daily 10.30am–7pm
Legendary stockist for famous English shoe brands including Dr Marten (since 1958) and Grinders. In the 1970s and 1980s the shop became a mecca for skinheads and punks from all over the world.

Camden Markets (B2-C2) ⑰
→ Chalk Farm Rd, NW1
Daily 10am–6pm
The most popular fleamarkets in town.
Buck Street Market
Open-air second-hand clothes market in Camden High Street; 200 stalls, along with record shops and punk stores.
Camden Lock Market
Ready-to-wear, craftware and accessories, along with exotic food stalls.
Stables Market
Furniture, antiques and fashion in converted stables (1854).
Regent's Park Road (A2) ⑱
Charming street lined with cafés, delis and stylish boutiques:
Graham & Green
→ 164 Regent's Park Road
Tel. 020 7586 2960
Mon-Sat 10am–6pm,
Sun 11.30am–5.30pm
Stylish furniture and homeware.
Mary's Living and Giving Shop
→ 109 Regent's Park Road
Tel. 020 7586 9666
Mon-Sat 10am–6pm;
Sun noon–5pm
Charity shop supporting the Save the Children charity, selling second-hand designer clothes.

...GY

BRITISH LIBRARY

LONDON CANAL MUSEUM

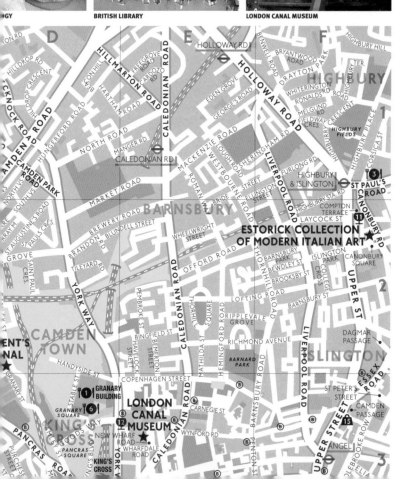

ESTORICK COLLECTION
OF MODERN ITALIAN ART

BARNSBURY

HIGHBURY

ISLINGTON

CAMDEN
TOWN

KING'S
CROSS

LONDON
CANAL
MUSEUM

GRANARY
BUILDING

► Map C

PRIMROSE HILL

KENWOOD HOUSE

...un 10am–4.30pm
...e warehouse built
...62 by Carlo Gatti
...7–78), an ice-cream
...ufacturer, has been
...erted into a museum
...g the history of
...in's inland waterways
...the life of the people
...lived on the boats.

**...storick Collection of
...ern Italian Art** (F2)
...ba Canonbury Square, N1
...020 7704 9522; Wed-Sat
...–6pm; Sun noon–5pm
...Georgian house
...lays the collection
...lian art belonging to
...Estorick (1913–93). On
... are key works by the
...eers of Futurism, a

movement inspired by
Cubism, speed and
technology – Boccioni,
Carrà, Severini, Russolo and
Balla – as well as paintings
by Modigliani, de Chirico
and Morandi.

★ **Regent's Canal** (D2)
Opened in 1820, this
8-mile canal links the
docks (**J** D2) to Paddington,
running along the north
side of Regent's Park
toward the leafy basin
of Little Venice (**F** E1).
The 3-mile walk along
the towpath from Camden
Lock is a real treat.

★ **Camden Town** (B2)
With old brick-built houses,
quaint shop windows, busy

street markets, music
shops, Punks and Goths,
and exotic smells, Camden
is a quirky and lively
district.

★ **Primrose Hill** (A2)
A short walk west of
Camden Town is a lovely
expanse of open space
with fine views over
London. The peace and
quiet of its grand Victorian
houses have led many
celebrities to settle here.

★ **London Zoo** (B3)
→ *Regent's Park, NW1; Daily
10am–6pm (4/5pm winter)*
Since opening in 1828, the
zoo has ceaselessly sought
to improve the wellbeing of
its animals, housed in 13

listed buildings over 36
acres. More than 750
species are represented,
from insects to giraffes,
including a splendid
collection of reptiles.

★ **Kenwood House** (A1)
→ *Hampstead Lane, NW3
(subway to Golders Green
station and bus no. 210)
Tel. 020 8348 1286
Daily 10am–5pm*
Nestling on Hampstead
Heath, this elegant house
(1766) contains works
by such Old Masters as
Rembrandt, Vermeer,
Gainsborough and Turner,
and portraits from the
Elizabethan era. Don't
miss the Adam Library.

WALLACE COLLECTION

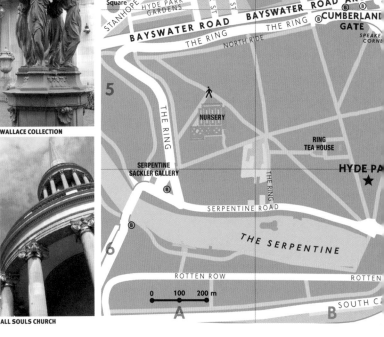

ALL SOULS CHURCH

E

★ **Regent's Park** (C1)
→ *Daily 5am–sunset*
In 1811, John Nash, already a famous architect, obtained the backing of the future King George IV to realize his dream of creating an idealized garden city on farmland once belonging to the Duke of Portland. Nash wanted terraces around the sides of the park with high porticos, tall stuccoed façades and massive colonnades. Inside he envisaged canals, lakes and grand mansions, with more modest houses clustered together around the perimeter. Only part of the project was realized,

but this superb green space has many other attractions including tennis courts, cricket pitches, a zoo, the Queen Mary Rose Garden and the Open Air Theater which stages outside productions every summer.

★ **Madame Tussauds** (C3)
→ *Marylebone Rd, NW1; Daily 9.30am–5.30pm (6pm Sat-Sun); Mid July-Aug 9am–7pm*
This famous waxworks museum is still the third most popular attraction in London. Next door, the former Planetarium houses the Marvel Superheroes 4D and Star Wars attractions.

★ **Sherlock Holmes Museum** (B3)
→ *221b Baker St, NW1*
Tel. 020 7224 3688
Daily 9.30am–6pm
Visitors are shown around the fictional super sleuth's Victorian apartments by his house-keeper, Mrs Hudson.

★ **Wallace Collection** (C4)
→ *Manchester Square, W1*
Tel. 020 7563 9500
Daily 10am–5pm
The 4th Marquess of Hertford (1800–70) was a dandy, an eccentric and a well-informed collector, passionately interested in painting (Hals, Fragonard, Rembrandt, Velasquez,

Poussin, Watteau), fur (Boulle and Riesener), objets d'art, and Easte and Western weaponr armor. His illegitimate Richard Wallace, cont to swell this priceless collection which was bequeathed to the Bri nation in 1897 on con that the works never l the museum.

★ **Handel & Hendri in London** (D4)
→ *25 Brook St, W1*
Tel. 020 7495 1685
Daily 11am (noon Sun)–
Two adjoining houses played host, 200 years apart, to two musician united by their genius

▶ Map D

REGENT'S PARK

MADAME TUSSAUDS

SHERLOCK HOLMES MUSEUM

ST JOHN'S
WOOD TERRACE
CHARLES LANE
ALLITSEN ROAD
EAMONT ST
CHARLBERT STREET

A

WELLINGTON ROAD
ST JOHN'S WOOD HIGH ST
COCHRANE ST
BRIDGEMAN ST
NEWCOURT ST

PRINCE ALBERT ROAD

REGENT'S CANAL

OUTER CIRCLE

B

1

CAVENDISH AVE

ST JOHN'S WOOD

WINFIELD HOUSE

LORD'S CRICKET GROUND

ST JOHN'S ROAD

OAK TREE ROAD

CENTRAL MOSQUE

PARK ROAD

OUTER CIRCLE

SYNAGOGUE

LODGE

NORTH BANK

PAVELEY STREET

BOATING LAKE

2

THRESHAM STREET

JEROME CRES

LISSON GROVE

CAPLAND ST

FRAMPTON STREET

LUTON ST

SAMFORD STREET

LILESTONE STREET

ROSSMORE RD

BOSTON ST

LINHOPE ST

BALCOMBE ST

GLOUCESTER PLACE

CHAGFORD ST

SHERLOCK HOLMES MUSEUM
★

PENFOLD STREET

CHURCH STREET

ASHBRIDGE ST

BROADLEY STREET

LISSON GROVE

HAREWOOD

19

MARYLEBONE STATION

MARYLEBONE

DORSET SQUARE

MELCOMBE STREET

EDGWARE ROAD

ASHMILL ST

SHROTON ST

COSWAY ST

BELL STREET

LISSON STREET

3

CHRIST CHURCH

MELCOMBE AVE

MELCOMBE PLACE

MARYLEBONE ROAD

DORSET SQUARE

3

NEWCASTLE PLACE

PENFOLD PLACE

CHARTER NIGHTINGALE HOSPITAL

SAMARITAN HOSPITAL

KNOX ST

UPPER MONTAGU ST

YORK STREET

BICKENHALL STREET

YORK

EDGWARE ROAD

ST MARY'S

CRAWFORD

GLOUCE

CHAPEL ST

TRANSEPT STREET

HARCOURT STREET

MARY

CARBELL ST

SHOULDHAM ST

MONTAGU SQ

PADDINGTON BASIN

EDGWARE ROAD

BRYANSTON PLACE

BRYANSTON SQ

MONTAGU

PRAED STREET

ST MICHAEL'S ST

STAR STREET

HARROWBY ST

NUTFORD PLACE

BROWN ST

BRYANSTON ST

BRYANSTON SQ

SEYMOUR PLACE

CUMBERLAND

GEORGE STREET

GREAT

4

NORFOLK CRES

CAMBRIDGE SQUARE

NORFOLK SQUARE

STOURCLIFFE STREET

UP. BERKELEY

MONTAGU

SUSSEX GARDENS

RADNOR

ST JOHNS

OXFORD SQUARE PLACE

PORCHESTER PLACE

STREET

10

Its name may derive from the 'May Fairs' (the local livestock and grain markets held here in the first week of May in the 17th century) but today Mayfair, with its prestigious hotels and luxury stores on New and Old Bond streets, is the classiest district in London. Marylebone, further north, is more lively, particularly around the High Street, with its striking Georgian façades and astonishing array of fashion stores and good restaurants. Around Regent's Park there are many neoclassical marvels, including John Nash's magnificent Cumberland Terrace, to the east of the park, with its blue and white pediment.

THE SEA SHELL

MAROUSH

RESTAURANTS

Nagomi (D4) ⑪❶
→ 4 Blenheim St, W1
Tel. 020 7165 9506; Mon-Fri noon–2.30pm, 6–10.30pm; Sat-Sun noon–3pm, 6–10.15pm (9.30pm Sun)
Authentic Japanese food in an informal, smart interior. Sushi, sashimi, tempura and teriyaki dishes. Entrées £8–24.

Carluccio's (C4) ⑫❷
→ St Christopher's Place, W1
Mon-Fri 7.30am–11.30pm; Sat-Sun 9am–10.30pm
One of Italian chef Antonio Carluccio's deli-restaurants. Prix fixe £11–14; entrées £9–16.

The Sea Shell (A3) ⑬❸
→ 49-51 Lisson Grove, NW1
Tel. 020 7224 9000
Mon-Fri noon–2.30pm, 5–10.30pm; Sat noon–10.30pm; Sun noon–6pm
Long-standing traditional fish & chip restaurant with black-and-white checkered floors and large marble counters; an institution. Takeout available. £13–33.

Maroush (B4) ⑭❹
→ 21 Edgware Rd, W2
Tel. 020 7723 0773
Daily noon–2am
The high quality of the cuisine in this Lebanese restaurant has not diminished since it opened in 1980; authentic and delicious mezze and grilled meats. Entrées £14–19.

Corrigan's Mayfair (C5) ⑮❺
→ 28 Upper Grosvenor St, W1; Tel. 020 7499 9943
Mon-Fri noon–3pm, 6–10pm; Sat 6–10pm; Sun noon–4pm
Modern British gourmet cuisine with dishes such as suckling pig cutlet with bok choy and medjool dates; and brown butter ice cream with caramelised apple. Exceptional wine list. Entrées £18–39. Reserve ahead.

Wild Honey (D5) ⑯❻
→ 12 St George St, W1
Tel. 020 7758 9160; Mon-Sat noon–2.30pm, 6–10.30pm
Seasonal, modern British fare in an elegant wood-paneled room: white truffle macaroni, saddle of rabbit, wild honey ice cream. Prix fixe (lunch) £29; entrées £32.
Its more casual sister restaurant is Arbutus (63 Frith St, B3).

TEAROOMS, CAFÉ

The Wallace (C4) ❼
→ Wallace Collection, Manchester Square, W1
Tel. 020 7563 9505; Daily

WIGMORE HALL

SOUTH MOLTON STREET

ALFIES ANTIQUE MARKET

10am–5pm (11pm Fri-Sat)
A gem of a tearoom (and French-style brasserie) at the heart of the museum, under a glass, light-filled atrium. Lovely cakes by Peyton and Byrne.

Rose Bakery (D5) **8**
→ 17-18 Dover St, W1
Tel. 020 7518 0687
Mon-Sat 11am–5pm;
Sun noon–4pm
On the top floor of the Dover Street Market: soups, vegetarian dishes, homemade cakes, fresh fruit juices and teas.

The Lanesborough (C6) **9**
→ Lanesborough Hotel, Hyde Park Corner, SW1
Tel. 020 7259 5599
Tea: daily 3–4.30pm
Afternoon tea at its most traditional in the conservatory of the 1828 hotel, across from Hyde Park. A top tea sommelier will guide you through the choice of teas.
£48–65.

BARS, MUSIC VENUE

Vinoteca (B4) **10**
→ 15 Seymour Place, W1
Tel. 020 7724 7288
Daily noon–11pm (4pm Sun)
The sister address of the original wine bar on St John St (**C** B1), offering

an extensive wine list, tasting evenings and bottles to take home at shop prices. Try over 20 different wines by the glass, with charcuterie and cheese boards.

The Social (D4) **11**
→ 5 Little Portland St, W1
Mon-Sat 11.30am–midnight (1am Thu-Sat);
Sun 6pm–1am
A small relaxed bar with great music, a juke box in the ground-floor bar and DJs downstairs from 6pm. Concerts and hip-hop karaoke.

Wigmore Hall (C4) **12**
→ 36 Wigmore St, W1
Tel. 020 7935 2141
Built in 1901, this small recital hall has wonderful acoustics. Excellent program of chamber music and jazz.

SHOPPING

Dover Street Market (D5) **13**
→ 17-18 Dover St, W1
Tel. 020 7518 0680
Mon-Sat 11am–6.30pm (7pm Thu-Sat);
Sun noon–6pm
Fascinating 'market' created by Rei Kawakubo showcasing the work of cutting-edge fashion designers; unisex clothing and accessories.

Geo F. Trumper (D5) **14**
→ 9 Curzon St, W1
Tel. 020 7499 1850; Mon-Sat 9am–5.30pm (5pm Sat)
Shaving brushes, razors, colognes, aftershaves: the last word in men's beauty products.

Topshop/ Topman (D4) **15**
→ 214 Oxford St, W1
Tel. 084 4848 7487
Mon-Sat 9.30am–10pm;
Sun 11.30am–6pm
Young fashion, with clothing, shoes, bags and accessories for men, women and children. Reasonable prices.

Old and New Bond Streets (D4-D5) **16**
The epitome of luxury shopping.
Smythson of Bond Street
→ New Bond St, W1
Luxury leather goods and accessories.
Alexander McQueen
→ Old Bond St, W1
The designer's latest creations for men and women.
De Beers; Tiffany
→ Old Bond Street, W1
Two of the most reputed jewelers in the world.
Charbonnel et Walker
→ 28 Old Bond Street
For the Queen's favorite chocolates.

South Molton Street (D4) **17**
Varied selection of stores: fashion, jewelery, accessories.
Browns Focus (no. 24)
The gutsy younger sister and next-door-neighbour of the more traditional Browns fashion store established in 1970. Hot-off-the-catwalk designs.
Hobbs (no. 47–48)
Classic womenswear, shoes and accessories.
Space NK (no. 47–48)
Skincare, fragrances, haircare, make up.

Selfridges (C4) **18**
→ 400 Oxford St, W1
Mon-Sat 9.30am–9pm;
Sun 11.30am–6pm
Huge, reputed department store stocking most fashion labels. Also bags, shoes, beauty products and gifts. The food hall, stocking specialty products, is renowned.

Alfies Antique Market (A2) **19**
→ 13-25 Church St, NW8
Tel. 020 7723 6066
Tue-Sat 10am–6pm
London's largest indoor market with four floors of antiques, vintage fashion, collectables and 20th-century design artefacts from all over the world.

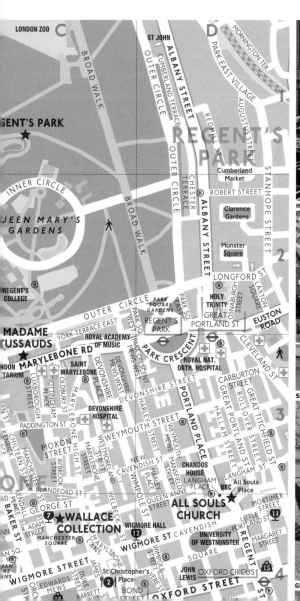

LONDON ZOO

ST JOHN

BROAD WALK

CUMBERLAND TERRACE
OUTER CIRCLE

ALBANY STREET

PARK EAST VILLAGE

MORNINGTON TER.

REDHILL ST

AUGUSTUS STREET

GENT'S PARK

REGENT'S PARK

INNER CIRCLE

OUTER CIRCLE

CHESTER TERRACE

ALBANY STREET

STANHOPE STREET

Cumberland Market

JEEN MARY'S GARDENS

BROAD WALK

ROBERT STREET

Clarence Gardens

Munster Square

REGENT'S COLLEGE

LONGFORD ST

LAXTON SQUARE

OUTER CIRCLE

PARK SQUARE GARDENS

PARK SQ WEST
PARK SQ EAST

HOLY TRINITY

OSNABURGH STREET

EUSTON ROAD

YORK TERRACE EAST

REGENT'S PARK

GREAT PORTLAND ST

MADAME TUSSAUDS

ROYAL ACADEMY OF MUSIC

PARK CRESCENT

CLEVELAND ST

NDON TARIUM

MARYLEBONE RD

PARK CRESCENT MEWS WEST

ROYAL NAT. ORTH. HOSPITAL

SAINT MARYLEBONE

DEVONSHIRE PLACE

CARBURTON STREET

OXBOROUGH

NOTTINGHAM PLACE

OLDBURY ST

DEVONSHIRE MEWS WEST

DEVONSHIRE STREET

BOLSOVER STREET

GREAT TITCHFIELD ST

GREAT PORTLAND STREET

DEVONSHIRE MEWS WEST

PADDINGTON STREET

MARYLEBONE HIGH ST

HARLEY STREET

PORTLAND PLACE

HALLAM STREET

DEVONSHIRE HOSPITAL

MARYLEBONE STREET

WEYMOUTH STREET

WEYMOUTH MEWS

MOXON STREET

WESTMORELAND STREET

AYBROOK STREET

NEW CAVENDISH ST

MANCHESTER STREET

WIMPOLE STREET

MANSFIELD STREET

CHANDOS HOUSE

LANGHAM ST

LANGHAM STREET

BLANDFORD ST

HARLEY PLACE

QUEEN ANNE PLACE

BBC

LANGHAM PLACE

All Souls Place

BAKER ST

KENDALL PLACE

GEORGE ST

WELBECK STREET

ALL SOULS CHURCH

MORTIMER STREET

R. ADAM STREET

MANCHESTER SQUARE

MARYLEBONE LANE

LITTLE PORTLAND ST

WALLACE COLLECTION

WIGMORE HALL

WIGMORE ST

CAVENDISH

UNIVERSITY OF WESTMINSTER

REGENT STREET

MARGARET STREET

WIGMORE STREET

WIMPOLE STREET

SQUARE

EVEREST ST

JOHN LEWIS

OXFORD CIRCUS

EDWARDS MEWS

JAMES STREET

DUKE STREET

St Christopher's Place

BOND ST

OXFORD STREET

WIGMORE STREET

BARRETT

HANDEL HOUSE MUSEUM

SHEPHERD MARKET

GREEN PARK

(map labels)
OXFORD STREET · SELFRIDGES · DUKE STREET · GILBERT ST · WEIGHOUSE STREET · SOUTH MOLTON ST · HANOVER ST · BLENHEIM ST · DERING ST · HANDEL & HENDRIX IN LONDON · CLARIDGE'S · LANCASHIRE COURT · BROOK STREET · DAVIES STREET · MADDOX ST · CONDUIT ST · SOTHEBY'S · ITALIAN EMBASSY · GROSVENOR ST · GROSVENOR HILL · BOND STREET · TIME AND LIFE BUILDING · CLIFFORD ST · U.S. EMBASSY · ROOSEVELT MEMORIAL · GROSVENOR SQUARE · CARLOS PL · MOUNT ROW · ADAM'S ROW · BROOK'S MEWS · BERKELEY ST · BRUTON ST · NEW BOND ST · GRAFTON ST · MOUNT STREET · REEVES MEWS · SOUTH AUDLEY ST · ALDFORD ST · IMMACULATE CONCEPTION · SOUTH ST · FARM STREET · HILL STREET · BERKELEY SQUARE GARDENS · HAY HILL · ALBEMARLE ST · OLD BOND ST · DORCHESTER · DEANERY ST · STANHOPE GATE · WAVERTON ST · HAY'S MEWS · QUEEN ST · CHARLES ST · STRATTON STREET · MAYFAIR PLACE · PARK LANE · SHEPHERD MARKET · CURZON STREET · WHITE HORSE ST · BOLTON STREET · CLARGES STREET · PICCADILLY · GREEN PARK · HERTFORD ST · DOWN ST · OLD PARK LANE · HAMILTON PL · ACHILLES' STATUE · APSLEY HOUSE · HYDE PARK CORNER · KNIGHTSBRIDGE · LANESBOROUGH HOTEL · CONSTITUTION HILL · BUCKINGHAM PALACE GARDENS · GREEN PARK · THE BROAD WALK · QUEEN VICTORIA MEMORIAL · PARK LANE · PARK LANE · ROAD · MAYFAR

APSLEY HOUSE

HYDE PARK

▲ Map G

---

for London. At no. 25,
private rooms occupied
Handel (1685–1759)
1723, with a recording
the original version of
Messiah; at no. 23,
home of Jimi Hendrix
(2–70) from 1968 to
9, restored to its former
e by his then girlfriend,
a personal items and
acoustic guitar.

All Souls Church (D4)
All Souls Place, W1
-Fri 9.30am–5.30pm;
8am–8.30pm
en it was completed in
4, this church, the only
built by John Nash that
stands, was likened by
he to a wedding cake.

★ **Shepherd Market** (D6)
→ Between Curzon St
and Piccadilly, W1
West of crowded Piccadilly,
this haven of peace
calls to mind a hamlet
threaded with pedestrian
streets and scattered
with paved courtyards. The
area used to be the center
of the May Fairs (trading
cereals and cattle) from
which the entire area
derived its name.

★ **Green Park** (D6)
Extensive lawns, shady
trees, cast-iron benches
and old gas lamps.
Originally a leper's burial
ground, no flowers are

planted out of respect
for those buried here.

★ **Apsley House** (C6)
→ Hyde Park Corner, W1
Tel. 020 7499 5676
Wed–Sun 10am–6pm
(4pm Sat–Sun Nov–March)
'Number One, London', as
the house is also known,
was given to the Duke of
Wellington (1769–1852) as
a reward for his victory over
Napoleon at the Battle of
Waterloo (1815). He was
also given many paintings
and precious objects
by influential figures,
a collection which he
enhanced with various
spoils of war. There are
paintings by great masters

(Velasquez, Goya, Rubens,
Caravaggio), sculpture
(Canova's *Naked Napoleon*),
silver and gold plate, and
priceless porcelain.

★ **Hyde Park** (B6)
→ Daily 5am–midnight
London's most popular
park is like an immense
green lung at the city's
center. Riders parade along
Rotten Row and bathers,
boats and swans play up
and down the Serpentine,
where a midnight swim is
held at Christmas. Since
1872, orators have aired
their opinions at Speaker's
Corner; anyone can stand
on a makeshift platform
and have their say here.

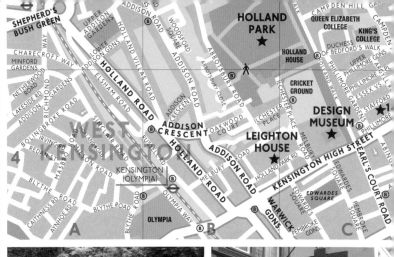

HOLLAND PARK

NOTTING HILL

★ **Kensington Gardens / Kensington Palace** (D3-E3)

→ *Palace: daily 10am–6pm (5pm Nov-Feb)*
Gardens: daily 6am–sunset
Originally a playground for the nation's young queens, the gardens are now a children's paradise with remote-controlled boats, puppet shows and a huge wooden pirate ship. The flower beds and water features in the Sunken Gardens are reminiscent of Tudor gardens. In 1689, King William III commissioned Christopher Wren and Nicholas Hawksmoor to enlarge the existing manor house and turn it into a royal palace. Between 1689 and 1837 all the British rulers lived and died there. Princess Victoria was baptized in the Cupola Room in 1819. The apartments have resplendent oak paneling and trompe-l'œil designs on the ceilings and walls.

★ **Serpentine Gallery** (F3)

→ *Kensington Gardens, W2*
Tel. 020 7402 6075
Tue-Sun 10am–6pm
A pretty former tea pavilion (1934) which hosts contemporary art exhibitions. The Serpentine Sackler Gallery (F3), an arts venue designed by Zaha Habib and housed in a Grade-II listed building, opened in 2013.

★ **Leighton House** (B4)

→ *12 Holland Park Rd, W14*
Tel. 020 7602 3316
Wed-Mon 10am–5.30pm
Extravagance reigns behind this classical façade. Frederic Leighton, artist and president of the Royal Academy, was a keen traveler and orientalist. The house is lavishly decorated and includes a priceless collection of faïence tiles from Iznik and a wonderful collection of pre-Raphaelite paintings by Leighton's contemporaries, including Burne-Jones and Milla...

★ **18 Stafford Terrace** (C4)

→ *18 Stafford Terrace, W...*
Tel. 020 7938 1295; Mid S...
mid June: Wed, Sat-Sun
2–5.30pm. Guided tours ...
A miraculously preserve...
Victorian interior where...
Punch cartoonist Edwa...
Linley Sambourne lived ...
from 1874 to 1910. The ...
are many examples of ...
caricatures on the wall ...
and most of the interio...
decoration is the work ...
craftsman William Mor...

★ **Design Museum**

→ *Kensington High St, W...*
Tel. 020 7403 6933
Daily 10am–5.45pm

SERPENTINE GALLERY

KENSINGTON GARDENS

Kensington, once an estate spread around the royal residence of Kensington Palace, has a split personality: it is both a busy shopping hub with many stores on Kensington High Street, and a prestigious residential area made up of mansion blocks and converted mews. To the north, the influx of wealthy newcomers to Notting Hill has gentrified the area and Golborne Road has acquired its share of hip eateries and stores. The long-standing Caribbean community, based to the north of Portobello Road, is as strong as ever, as evidenced by the Notting Hill Carnival every August. To the east the canals of Little Venice are ideal for a stroll.

MAGGIE JONES'S

OTTOLENGHI

RESTAURANTS

Taqueria (C2) 🍽️❶
→ 139 Westbourne Grove, W11; Daily noon–11pm (11.30pm Fri-Sat; 10.30pm Sun)
This small Mexican diner has an extensive menu of *sopas, tostadas*, tacos and homemade, soft corn tortillas. Entrées £5–8.

Electric Diner (B1) 🍽️❷
→ 191 Portobello Rd, W11 Daily 8am–midnight (2am Fri-Sat, 11pm Sun)
The eatery of the Electric Cinema movie theater. American classics (burgers, hot dogs, milkshakes) in an atmospheric setting with red leather banquettes and an open kitchen. Entrées £9–17.

John Doe (B1) 🍽️❸
→ 46 Golborne Road, W10 Tel. 020 8969 3280; Tue-Sun noon–midnight (4pm Sun)
This restaurant, decorated with white tiles and wood trim, uses local ingredients supplied from sustainable sources and cooks them in a coal-fired oven. Game in various formats (burgers, tartare), roast pigeon, duck's heart, crab – and craft beer. Entrées £10–23.

Kateh (E1) 🍽️❹
→ 5 Warwick Place, W9

Tel. 020 7289 3393 Mon-Thu 6–11pm; Fri-Sat noon–4pm, 6–11pm; Sun noon–9.30pm
Slightly off the beaten track, by the canals of Little Venice, this pretty restaurant offers a modern, fresh take on Persian cuisine, including vegetarian dishes. £12–20.

The Cow (C1) 🍽️❺
→ 89 Westbourne Park Rd, W2; Tel. 020 7221 0021 Mon-Sat 7–11pm; Sun noon–3.30pm. Bar: Daily noon–11pm (10.30pm Sun)
A fashionable Notting Hill hangout with a busy Irish bar serving Guinness and fresh oysters and a quieter gastropub upstairs with an accent on seafood. Entrées £10 (lunch), £14–23 (dinner).

Maggie Jones's (D3) 🍽️❻
→ 6 Old Court Place, W8 Tel. 020 7937 6462; Daily noon–2.30pm, 6–10.30pm
This three-story, quirky restaurant looks like an old farmhouse, with wooden floorboards and snug alcoves. Simple, quality British fare: saddle of lamb, steak and kidney pie, bread and butter pudding. Entrées £9 (lunch), £15–29 (dinner).

CHILL ARMS

NOTTING HILL ARTS CLUB

CERAMICA BLUE

TEAROOM, CAFÉS

The Orangery (D3) **7**
→ Kensington Palace, W8
Tel. 020 3166 6113; Daily
10am–6pm (5pm in winter)
What better setting for
traditional high tea than
this large, light and airy
glass house designed
by Sir John Vanbrugh
for Queen Anne in 1704.
Afternoon tea £26–36
per person.

Ottolenghi (C2) **8**
→ 63 Ledbury Rd, W11
Tel. 020 7727 1121; Mon-Sat
8am–8pm (7pm Sat);
Sun 9am–6pm
The first in Ottolenghi's
empire, and seating
only ten people, this is
mainly a takeout place.
The windows display an
array of cakes, meringues
and colorful dishes
drawing on Middle
Eastern flavors.

**Daylesford Organic
Café** (C2) **9**
→ 208-212 Westbourne Grove
Tel. 020 7313 8050
Mon-Sat 8am–9.30pm
(7pm Mon); Sun 10am–4pm
Soups, salads, freshly
baked bread and
puddings on offer in
this spacious, airy café,
which also has a deli
selling farm produce.
Attractive terrace, open
to the sunshine.

PUBS, MOVIE
THEATER, CLUB

Churchill Arms (C3) **10**
→ 119 Kensington
Church St, W8; Tel. 020 7727
4242; Mon-Sat 11am–11pm;
Sun noon–10.30pm
A visually striking pub
where the walls and
ceilings are hung with
wicker baskets, utensils,
paintings and photos; the
best part – the excellent
Thai food. Reserve.

Ladbroke Arms
(C2) **11**
→ 54 Ladbroke Rd, W11
Mon-Sat 11.30am–11pm;
Sun noon–10.30pm
A cozy, classy pub in a
little house off the main
street, with open fires,
comfy seating and good
pub food. Small terrace
in summer.

**Electric
Cinema** (B2) **12**
→ 191 Portobello Rd, W11
electriccinema.co.uk
This movie theater
(the first in London,
dating from 1911) has
comfy two-seater sofas
(reserve in advance) with
footstools and side tables
for snacks from the bar...
and cashmere blankets
no less! Mainstream and
art-house program. The
Electric Diner next door
is open all day.

**Notting Hill Arts
Club** (D2) **13**
→ 21 Notting Hill Gate, W11
Tue-Sat 7pm–2am
nottinghillartsclub.com
A basement club
featuring alternative
world music including
Latino funk, Asian drum
'n' bass and Gypsy punk.

SHOPPING

**Fara Kids &
Baby** (C2) **14**
→ 39-41 Ledbury Rd, W11
Tel. 020 7229 3634
Daily 10am–6pm
Charity shop exclusively
for youngsters, with
clothes and accessories
from famous names in
children's fashion.

Rellik (off map B1) **15**
→ 8 Golborne Rd, W10
Tel. 020 8962 0089
Tue-Sat 10am–6pm
One of the best vintage
clothes stores in London,
opened by three former
dealers from Portobello
Road.

Rough Trade (B1) **16**
→ 130 Talbot Rd
Tel. 020 7229 8541
Mon-Sat 10am–6.30pm;
Sun 11am–5pm
This record store was a
key player in the punk
movement, and its
label, founded in 1976,
launched groups such

as the Smiths. Its eclectic
stock now ranges far
beyond Indie rock.
There are also in-store
performances.

Paul Smith (B2) **17**
→ Westbourne House, 122
Kensington Park Rd, W11
Tel. 020 7727 353; Mon-Sat
10am–6pm (6.30pm Sat);
Sun noon–5pm
The flagship store of
this bastion of British
men's fashion, situated
in a grand Edwardian
mansion. Classic cuts
and exquisite fabrics with
retro and ethnic touches.

**Books for
Cooks** (B1) **18**
→ 4 Blenheim Crescent, W11
Tue-Sat 10am–6pm
(5.30pm Thu)
A heaven for foodies,
with cookbooks from
floor to ceiling and a
kitchen at the back which
tries out recipes for lunch.
The Spice Shop, at no. 1
on the same street, has
the aromatic herbs,
spices and dried fruits to
realize the recipes.

Ceramica Blue (B1) **19**
→ 10 Blenheim Crescent,
W11; Mon-Sat 10am–
6.30pm; Sun noon–5pm
The tableware, tiles and
giftware here are the work
of potters from different
countries; super colors
and craftsmanship.

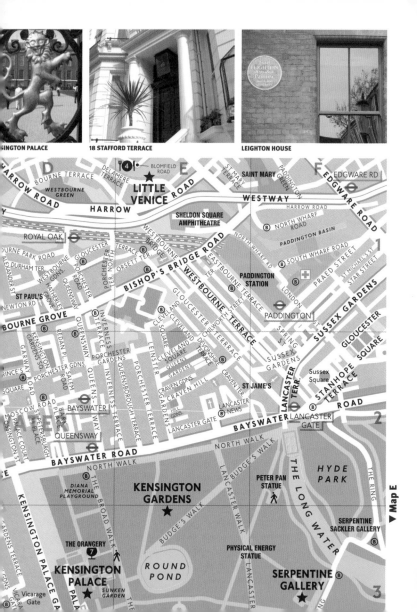

KENSINGTON PALACE

18 STAFFORD TERRACE

LEIGHTON HOUSE

D

HARROW ROAD

BOURNE TERRACE

WESTBOURNE GREEN

ROYAL OAK

OURNE PARK ROAD

DURHAM TER.

ALEXANDER ST

ST PAUL'S

NEWTON RD

BOURNE GROVE

PRINCE'S SQUARE

GARWAY ROAD

SQUARE

MOSCOW ROAD

PALACE COURT

KENSINGTON ST

ST PETERSBURGH PLACE

BARK PLACE

E

DELAMERE TERRACE

BLOMFIELD ROAD

4

LITTLE VENICE

HARROW

SHELDON SQUARE AMPHITHEATRE

WESTBOURNE TERRACE

WESTBOURNE BRIDGE

TER. NORTH

BISHOP'S BRIDGE ROAD

ORSETT TER.

WESTBOURNE TERRACE

WESTBOURNE PARK ROAD

GLOUCESTER TERRACE

GLOUCESTER TERRACE

CHILWORTH STREET

EASTBOURNE TER.

CLEVELAND TERRRACE

DEVONSHIRE TERRACE

CLEVELAND SQUARE

CLEVELAND GARDENS

LEINSTER SQUARE

QUEENSWAY

HATHERLEY

QUEENSWAY

PORCHESTER GDNS.

REDAN PL.

INVERNESS TERRACE

PORCHESTER GARDENS

QUEENS-WAY

INVERNESS TERRACE

SALEM ROAD

PORCHESTER TERRACE

QUEENSBOROUGH TERRACE

CRAVEN GDNS.

CRAVEN HILL GARDENS

HILL GDNS.

LANCASTER GATE

CRAVEN HILL

CRAVEN TER.

ST JAMES'S

LANCASTER NEWS

BAYSWATER

QUEENSWAY

BAYSWATER ROAD

NORTH WALK

DIANA MEMORIAL PLAYGROUND

THE BROAD WALK

KENSINGTON GARDENS ★

BUDGE'S WALK

THE ORANGERY **7**

KENSINGTON PALACE

KENSINGTON PALACE GA

GARDENS TERRACE

Vicarage Gate

SUNKEN GARDEN

PALA

ROUND POND

BUDGE'S WALK

LANCASTER WALK

NORTH WALK

BAYSWATER

LANCASTER GATE

F

SAINT MARY

ST MARY TERRACE

EDGWARE RD

EDGWARE ROAD

WESTWAY

HARROW ROAD

NORTH WHARF ROAD

PADDINGTON BASIN

NORTH WHARF RD.

SOUTH WHARF ROAD

PADDINGTON STATION

PRAED STREET

ST MICHAEL'S ST.

STAR STREET

LONDON ST.

PADDINGTON

SPRING ST

SUSSEX GARDENS

SUSSEX GARDENS

GLOUCESTER SQUARE

LANCASTER TERR.

Sussex Square

STANHOPE TERRACE

GLOUCESTER SQUARE

ROAD

BAYSWATER

LANCASTER GATE

1

2

PETER PAN STATUE ⚓

HYDE PARK

THE RING

SERPENTINE SACKLER GALLERY ⑧

PHYSICAL ENERGY STATUE

SERPENTINE GALLERY ★

THE LONG WATER

LANCASTER

▼ Map E

3

Map showing Kensington area with streets including Kensington High St, Kensington Road, Prince Consort Rd, Exhibition Road, Cromwell Road, Queen's Gate, Gloucester Road. Landmarks: Albert Memorial, Royal Albert Hall, Imperial College of Science and Technology, British Museum of Natural History, Victoria and Albert Museum, High Street Kensington station.

BELLO ROAD MARKET

MUSEUM OF BRANDS

LITTLE VENICE

rmer Commonwealth ute building (1962) een renovated by the nalist architect John on, providing 108,000 of extra space for the rn Museum (**I** F2) to ay its collection of ts (telephones, s, washing machines, lating from the 19th ry to the present day. itions, workspaces ung designers and al signposting by the dge Levene studio.

olland Park (B3) ily 7.30am–sunset nost romantic and ely wooded of on's parks comprises

a group of small gardens which are home to peacocks. All that remains of Holland House (1605), the Dutch-style manor house to which these lands once belonged, is the west wing, a rare vestige of the Jacobean period. Plays, ballets and operas are performed on the terrace.

★ **Notting Hill** (B2)
Notting Hill, a somewhat neglected district until the 1990s, became popular with young wealthy professionals looking for a Bohemian environment. Georgian houses stand on the higher ground and streets on

the slopes are lined with pastel houses. Spectacular 3-day festival in August.
★ **Portobello Road Market** (C2)
→ *Portobello / Golborne rds, W11; Mon-Sat 9am–6pm (1pm Thu, 7pm Fri-Sat)*
This huge market is a must on Saturdays, with fruit and vegetable stalls, antiques, second-hand clothes, jewelry and bric-a-brac.
★ **Museum of Brands, Packaging and Advertising** (A1)
→ *111-117 Lancaster Road, W11 Tel. 020 7243 961; Tue-Sat 10am–6pm; Sun 11am–5pm*
A collection of everyday products displayed by

decade, from the Victorian era to the present. This is a history of the consumer society featuring packaging, posters and samples of long-forgotten but once familiar items.
★ **Little Venice** (E1)
→ *Puppet Theatre Barge, Blomfield Road, W9*
At the junction of the Grand Union Canal and Regent's Canal is a large basin where narrowboats can manoeuvre to moor along the sides of a short third canal. These days all the boats are pleasure craft and houseboats. Don't miss the charming floating puppet theater.

CHRISTIE'S

CHELSEA PHYSIC GARDEN

★ **Royal Albert Hall** (B1)
→ Kensington Gore, SW7
Tel. 0845 401 5034; guided tours: royalalberthall.com
The famous red-brick hall with its wrought-iron, glazed dome (1871) owes its reputation to the Proms, a series of classical music concerts held each summer, but it also stages pop and jazz concerts. Across the road, in Kensington Gardens, is the Albert Memorial, commissioned by Queen Victoria after the early death of her husband in 1861, and designed by Sir George Gilbert Scott in the Gothic Revival style.

★ **Brompton Oratory** (C2)
→ Brompton Rd, SW7
Daily 6.30am–8pm
This neo-Baroque Catholic church (1884) houses 12 statues of the apostles by G. Mazzuoli (1644–1725) which once stood in the cathedral in Siena, Italy.

★ **Victoria & Albert Museum** (C2)
→ Cromwell Rd, SW7
Tel. 020 7942 2000; Daily 10am–5.45pm (10pm Fri)
The V&A holds the largest collection of decorative arts in the world. Four million pieces are on display in 146 rooms: European and Asiatic objects including Raphael's Cartoons, Indian fabrics, Korean ceramics and a section on Indian art that is unmatched outside India. Fifteen British galleries tell the story of British design from the reign of Henry VIII to that of Queen Victoria. There is also sculpture, paintings and photographs, as well as temporary exhibitions.

★ **Science Museum** (C1)
→ Exhibition Rd, SW7
Tel. 020 7942 4000
Daily 10am–6pm
A museum at the cutting edge of scientific progress. Interactive displays and simulations abound on the four floors, a wonderful showcase for the lates[...] in scientific developme[...] (the most recent missi[...] Mars, advances in gen[...] engineering, etc). The [...] rooms focus on the lea[...] inventions of the indus[...] era, such as George Stephenson's Rocket, a V2 missile and the Ap[...] 10 command module.

★ **Natural History Museum** (B2)
→ Cromwell Rd, SW7
Tel. 020 7942 5000
Daily 10am–5.50pm
Even the façade of this fascinating museum – one of Europe's largest is swarming with plants There are 78 million

G

ROYAL ALBERT HALL

BROMPTON ORATORY

VICTORIA & ALBERT MUSEUM

▶ Map F

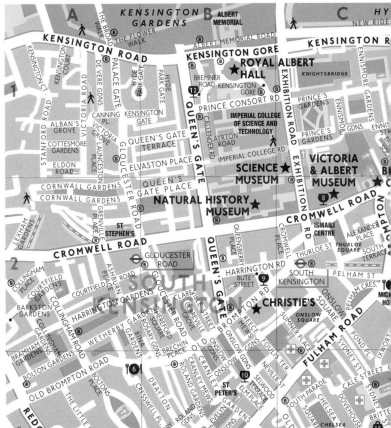

G

This area exudes stylish elegance: from South Kensington's world-class museums to Knightsbridge, epicenter of luxury shopping with Harrods and Sloane Street, the showcase of haute couture. Further east, embassies and aristocratic residences are ensconced behind the impressive façades of Belgravia, a world away from the lively village atmosphere of Chelsea. Here you can give free rein to extravagant impulses in the boutiques and inviting cafés, or enjoy a more economical stroll past antique stores and along the pretty streets which, before World War Two, were home to penniless artists.

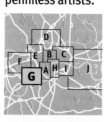

THE PHOENIX

BIBENDUM

RESTAURANTS

The Phoenix (D3) ❶
→ 23 Smith St, SW3
Tel. 020 7730 9182
Mon-Sat 11am–11pm;
Sun noon–10.30pm
A fine gourmet gastropub, with a lovely terrace and traditional pub food. Occasional specialty game menu, and fish & chips every Friday. Entrées £6–9 (lunch), £11–16 (dinner).

Pig's Ear (C4) ❷
→ 35 Old Church St, SW3
Tel. 020 7352 2908
Mon-Fri noon–3pm,
6–10pm; Sat-Sun noon–10pm (9pm Sun). Bar: daily noon–midnight (11pm Sun)
Modern British food at its best – pork belly with apple chutney, sticky toffee and date pudding, traditional Sunday roasts – in the ground floor bar or upstairs in the dining room. Entrées £12–22.

The Thomas Cubitt (F2) ❸
→ 44 Elizabeth St, SW1
Tel. 020 7730 6060
Restaurant: daily noon–3pm, 6–10pm (9.30pm Sun)
This Belgravia institution doubles as a restaurant and an upmarket pub: roast lamb, beef and Guinness pie, venison stew, fish & chips.

Entrées £15–48.
Amaya (E1) ❹
→ 15 Halkin Arcade,
Motcomb St, SW1
Tel. 020 7823 1166
Daily 12.30–2.15pm, 6.30–11.30pm (10.30pm Sun)
The same owners as Chutney Mary and Masala Zone. Here sophisticated Indian cuisine is served in a sultry interior. The menu specializes in small portions cooked on the sigree grill, on the tawa griddle or in the tandoor oven. Entrées £16–43.

Bibendum (C2) ❺
→ Michelin House,
81 Fulham Rd, SW3
Tel. 020 7581 5817
Daily noon–2.15pm, 7–10.30pm
A former tire factory magnificently converted, with amazing Art Deco stained-glass windows. Excellent cuisine – classic French with a British influence. The oyster bar on the ground floor is more affordable than the restaurant. Three-course lunch prix fixe (Sundays) £33.50; entrées £17–36.

Cambio de Tercio (A3) ❻
→ 163 Old Brompton Rd,
SW5; Tel. 020 7244 8970
Mon-Sat noon–2.30pm, 6.30–11.30pm; Sun noon–3pm, 6.30–11pm

ANGLESEA ARMS

HARRODS

CATH KIDSTON

Mouthwatering choice of tapas for starters (clams, squid, Galician octopus) and perfect paellas. Excellent wine list. Tapa £9–13; entrées £24–28.

Marcus (E1) 🍴
→ The Berkeley Hotel, Wilton Place, SW1
Tel. 020 7235 1200; Mon-Sat noon–2.45pm, 6–10.45pm
Lauded as one of the most talented British chefs, Marcus Wareing's take on classic French cuisine at his Michelin-starred restaurant will make for an exceptional meal. His custard tart is a favorite since he cooked it for the Queen. Prix fixe £55 (lunch); entrées £85–£105.

ICE-CREAM PARLOR, CAFÉ

V&A Café (C2) 🔟
→ Victoria & Albert Museum, Cromwell Rd, SW7
Tel. 020 7942 2000; Daily 10am–5.15pm (9.30pm Fri)
A historic setting for this lavish gallery-café and a choice of three magnificent rooms with decorated fireplaces, high ceilings, tiled walls and grand chandeliers. If you are lucky, you may have some piano or harp

accompaniment.

Oddono's (B2) 🟡
→ 14 Bute St, SW7
Mon-Thu, Sun 10am–11pm; Fri-Sat 9.30am–midnight
Fabulous Italian homemade ice creams and sorbets in a wide range of flavors. Soya-based and no-added-sugar options available.

PUBS, BAR

The Anglesea Arms (B3) 🔟
→ 15 Selwood Terrace, SW7
Mon-Sat 11am–11pm; Sun noon–10.30pm
A picture-perfect English gastropub with floral wallpaper, etched glass and wood partitions that create private alcoves. Charles Dickens once lived on the same street.

Fox and Hounds (E2) 🔟
→ 29 Passmore St, SW1
Tel. 020 7730 6367
Daily noon–11pm
This small, cozy pub is traditional in the best sense of the word, with wood panel decor and a distinctly British feel.

Bar 190 (B1) 🔟
→ Gore Hotel, 190 Queen's Gate, SW7
Daily noon–1.30am
A hotel bar with red wood paneling, colonial-style

decor and plush sofas. Ideal for a drink after a visit to one of the many museums nearby.

SHOPPING

Harrods (D1) 🔟
→ 87-135 Brompton Rd, SW1
Mon-Sat 10am–9pm; Sun 11.30am–6pm
Founded by tea merchant Henry Charles Harrod in 1849, Harrods is London's most famous department store. The stunning Food Halls are the last word in luxury food, wines and gourmet hampers.

Harvey Nichols (E1) 🔟
→ Knightsbridge, SW1
Mon-Sat 10am–8pm; Sun 11.30am–6pm
The stylish 'Harvey Nics' department store, dating from 1831, has the edge on Harrods for designer collections. Restaurants and café on the fifth floor.

Chelsea Farmers Market (C3) 🔟
→ Sydney St, SW3
Daily 10am–7pm
A community market selling good-quality locally grown food, artisan products, flowers and plants from small multicolored wooden huts.

British Red Cross Shop (C3) 🔟
→ 69-71 Old Church St, SW3
Tel. 020 7376 7300
Mon-Sat 10am–6pm
A stylish charity shop in a salubrious street, filled to bursting with vintage items and clothes by top designers (among them, Alexander McQueen and Vivienne Westwood) and prestigious labels (Gucci, Prada, Jaeger etc).

Cath Kidston (C3) 🔟
→ 27 King's Rd, SW3
Tel. 020 7259 9847
Mon-Sat 10am–7pm; Sun 11am–5pm
Flowers, stars, strawberries, peas.. these are the colourful motifs adorning this designer's bags, rain boots, household items and picnic ware.

Brora (C3) 🔟
→ 344 King's Rd, SW3
Mon-Sat 10am–6pm; Sun noon–5pm; other locations in London (see brora.co.uk)
A Scottish company selling cashmere clothing, accessories and baby products renowned for their subtly blended shades. The cashmere is made in the owners' mill in Scotland, which has been producing the wool for over 200 years.

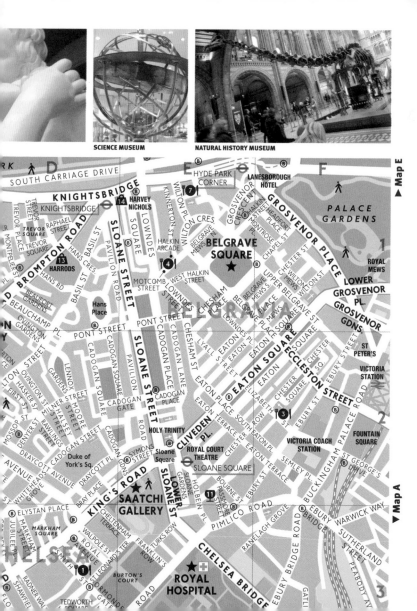

SCIENCE MUSEUM

NATURAL HISTORY MUSEUM

▲ Map E

RK · D

SOUTH CARRIAGE DRIVE

E · HYDE PARK CORNER

LANESBOROUGH HOTEL

F

KNIGHTSBRIDGE

KNIGHTSBRIDGE

HARVEY NICHOLS

PALACE GARDENS

TREVOR STREET
TREVOR PLACE
TREVOR SQUARE
RAPHAEL STREET
MONTPELIER ST

SLOANE STREET

SLOANE AVENUE

LOWNDES SQUARE

KINNERTON PL

WILTON PL

GROSVENOR CRESCENT

HALKIN ST
HEADFORT PLACE
MONTROSE PL

GROSVENOR PLACE

ROYAL MEWS

1

HANS CRES
BASIL ST

HALKIN ARCADE

BELGRAVE MEWS

BELGRAVE SQUARE

CHAPEL ST

WILTON CRES

CHESTER ST

LOWER GROSVENOR PL.

BROMPTON ROAD

HARRODS

HANS RD
BASIL ST

MOTCOMB STREET
WEST HALKIN STREET
LOWNDES STREET

BELGRAVE PLACE
UPPER BELGRAVE ST
BELGRAVE MEWS S.

WILTON ST

GROSVENOR GDNS.

BEAUFORT GARDENS

OVINGTON GARDENS

Hans Place

BELGRAVIA

ST PETER'S

BEAUCHAMP PL.

PONT STREET

CHESHAM STREET

EATON PL

LOWNDES PL

LYALL STREET

EATON MEWS

EATON SQUARE

EATON SQUARE

VICTORIA STATION

OVINGTON STREET

PONT STREET

CADOGAN LANE
CHESHAM ST

EATON PLACE

EATON TERRACE

EATON

ELIZABETH ST

CHESTER ROW

ECCLESTON STREET

EBURY STREET

EBURY STREET

ST PETER'S

LENNOX GARDENS
CADOGAN SQUARE

PAVILION ROAD

CADOGAN PLACE

SOUTH EATON PL

CHESTER SQUARE

CHESTER SQ.

HASKER ST
MILNER STREET
MOORE STREET
HALSEY ST
DENYER ST
RAWLINGS

CADOGAN GATE

CADOGAN PLACE

EATON TERRACE
EATON MEWS S.

SOUTH EATON PL

CHESTER ST

FOUNTAIN SQUARE

MOSSOP ST
DRAYCOTT AVENUE
CADOGAN STREET

SYMONS STREET

HOLY TRINITY

CLIVEDEN PL.

SEMLEY PL.

VICTORIA COACH STATION

BUCKINGHAM PALACE ROAD

ST GEORGE'S DRIVE

DRAYCOTT PL.

Sloane Square

ROYAL COURT THEATRE

CHESTER EATON TERRACE

FIRST ST

Duke of York's Sq

BRAY PLACE

SLOANE SQUARE

WHITEHEADS GROVE

KING'S ROAD

SAATCHI GALLERY

LOWER SLOANE ST

HOLBEIN PL.

BOURNE ST
PASSMORE

PIMLICO ROAD

RANELAGH GROVE

EBURY ST
EBURY BRIDGE ROAD

BRIDGE

WARWICK WAY

SUTHERLAND STREET

AVENUE

SLOANE GDNS
SLODENS

ELYSTAN PLACE

MARKHAM STREET

MARKHAM SQUARE

CHELTENHAM TERRACE

WALPOLE ST
FRANKLIN'S ROW
TURKS ROW

JUBILEE

ROYAL AVENUE

ST LEONARDS TER

BURTON'S COURT

CHELSEA BRIDGE

ROYAL HOSPITAL

EBURY BRIDGE ROAD

GATLI

PEABODY AV

CHELSEA

SMITH ST

RADNOR WA

SHAWFIELD

TEDWORTH

FLO

ROYAL

ST LEONARDS ST

ORMONDE GATE

ROAD

3

▲ Map A

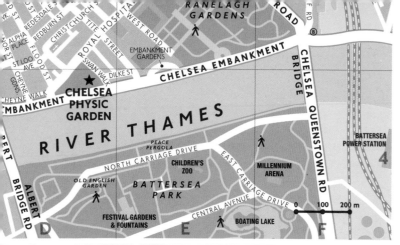

CHRISTCHURCH ST
TITE HOSPITAL
ROYAL STREET
WEST ROAD
RANELAGH GARDENS
F RD
CHEYNE GDNS
SWAN WALK
DILKE ST
EMBANKMENT GARDENS

★ **CHELSEA PHYSIC GARDEN**

CHELSEA EMBANKMENT

CHELSEA BRIDGE

CHELSEA QUEENSTOWN RD

RIVER THAMES

BATTERSEA POWER STATION

PEACE PERGOLA

NORTH CARRIAGE DRIVE

EAST CARRIAGE DRIVE

CHILDREN'S ZOO

MILLENNIUM ARENA

OLD ENGLISH GARDEN

BATTERSEA PARK

CENTRAL AVENUE

EAST CARRIAGE DRIVE

0   100   200 m

FESTIVAL GARDENS & FOUNTAINS

BOATING LAKE

ALBERT BRIDGE RD

D   E   F   4

HOSPITAL

SAATCHI GALLERY

BELGRAVE SQUARE

mens here, but only a part of the collection hibited, charting the ry and diversity of life rth, from dinosaurs to quakes. A skating rink up in the forecourt Nov-Jan.

hristie's (B2)
Old Brompton Rd, SW7
20 7930 6074; Tue-Sun
(11am Sat-Sun)–5pm
he illustrious dealer, ded in 1766, where s d'art and other s are auctioned.

helsea Physic en (D4)
Royal Hospital Rd,
Tel. 020 7352 5646
Oct: Tue-Fri, Sun

11am–6pm; Nov-March:
Mon-Fri 10am–4pm
The oldest botanical garden in England, along with that in Oxford, it was founded in 1673 by the Apothecaries' Company, which wanted medicinal plants for scientific study. Through the centuries the garden grew more exotic species, thanks to gifts by, most notably, Sir Hans Sloane. Today there are more than 7,000 varieties of vegetables, herbs, fruits and many centenary trees.
★ Royal Hospital (E3)
→ Royal Hospital Rd, SW3
Tel. 020 7881 5200; Mon-Fri
10am–4pmGuided tours:

10am and 1.30pm by reservation 1 month ahead
The Chelsea Flower Show is held in May in the gardens of this army retirement home founded by Charles II in the 17th century. Its 400 Chelsea Pensioners, in 18th-century uniform, wear a tricorn hat on special occasions. The chapel and refectory are open to visitors.
★ Saatchi Gallery (E2)
→ Duke of York's HQ, King's
Rd, SW3; Tel. 020 7811 3070
Daily 10am–6pm
The world's largest private gallery of contemporary art, belonging to art collector

Charles Saatchi, whose sponsorship has launched the career of many British artists. Set in beautiful premises, the staggering 70,000 sq. ft of exhibition space are dedicated to British modern art and to the works of contemporary foreign artists rarely seen in the UK. Entry is free.
★ Belgrave Square (E1)
This very orderly district was designed in 1824 by Thomas Cubitt (1788–1855). Beautifully proportioned brick and white-stuccoed Victorian buildings, which are so typical of Chelsea, border the square.

BFI SOUTHBANK

**SOUTHBANK CENTRE /
ROYAL FESTIVAL HALL**

★ Blackfriars Bridge (D1)

Beneath this colorful bridge with its wrought iron arches, a series of carvings illustrate the history of the surrounding area and the role played by the River Thames. The present structure dates from 1869, but a bridge has stood on this spot since 1769. At that time it was the third to straddle the river: until 1738, London Bridge was the only bridge connecting the two banks.

★ OXO Tower (C2)

→ *Barge House St, SE1*
In the 1920s this old power station became a cold store for Liebig, the manufacturer of the famous OXO stock cubes. It has now been refurbished as an apartment block in Art Deco style, complete with retail outlets, art galleries, a panoramic restaurant and a tower with luminous red letters that stand out on the skyline.

★ National Theatre (B2)

→ *South Bank, SE1*
Tel. 020 7452 3400
Guided tours: Daily 10am–5pm by reservation (nationaltheatre.org.uk)
One of the most acclaimed theaters in the city, this concrete building, designed by Denys Lasdun in 1975, has three auditoriums staging everything from avant-garde plays to spectacular musicals. Guided tours (starting in the main hall that also mounts exhibitions of contemporary art) take you backstage for a fascinating look at the stage machinery.

★ BFI Southbank (B2)

→ *South Bank, SE1*
Tel. 020 7928 3232
Mediatheque: Tue-Sun noon (12.30pm Sat-Sun, 1pm Tue)–8pm; Reuben Library: Tue-Sat 10.30am–7pm
The British Film Institute is the temple of cinema in London, with four screens for movies, retrospectives, talks and major events such as the London Film Festival in the fall. Its Reuben Library holds the world's largest collection of information on film and television.

★ Southbank Centre (B2)

→ *Belvedere Rd, South Bank, SE1; Tel. 020 7960 4200*
Daily 10am–11pm
Its critics felt that the chic gray concrete shouldn't have been left without adornment when this artistic center was built in 1951. A major program of renovation has led to the opening of cafés and restaurants along the

BLACKFRIARS BRIDGE

OXO TOWER

NATIONAL THEATRE

▶ **Map B**

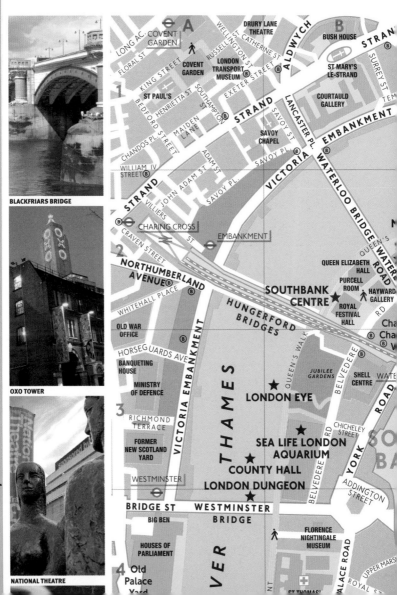

LONG AC. COVENT GARDEN

A

FLORAL ST

KING STREET

COVENT GARDEN

WELLINGTON ST

ST CATHERINE ST

DRURY LANE THEATRE

ALDWYCH

RUSSELL STREET

EXETER STREET

B

BUSH HOUSE

STRAN

ST MARY'S LE-STRAND

SURREY ST

ST PAUL'S

BEDFORD STREET

HENRIETTA ST

SOUTHAMPTON

LONDON TRANSPORT MUSEUM

STRAND

COURTAULD GALLERY

TEM

1

MAIDEN LANE

ADAM ST

SAVOY ST

LANCASTER PL.

EMBANKMENT

SAVOY CHAPEL

CHANDOS PL.

WILLIAM IV STREET

JOHN ADAM ST

SAVOY PL.

SAVOY PL.

VICTORIA EMBANKMENT

WATERLOO BRIDGE ROAD

STRAND

VILLIERS

CHARING CROSS

EMBANKMENT

QUEEN'S

CRAVEN STREET

ST

2

NORTHUMBERLAND AVENUE

WATER

QUEEN ELIZABETH HALL

WHITEHALL PLACE

HUNGERFORD BRIDGES

SOUTHBANK CENTRE

PURCELL ROOM

HAYWARD GALLERY

OLD WAR OFFICE

ROYAL FESTIVAL HALL

RD

HORSE GUARDS AVE.

Cha

Cha

V

BANQUETING HOUSE

QUEEN'S WALK

BELVEDERE

JUBILEE GARDENS

SHELL CENTRE

WATE

MINISTRY OF DEFENCE

THAMES

3

RICHMOND TERRACE

VICTORIA EMBANKMENT

LONDON EYE

ROAD

CHICHELEY STREET

SO

FORMER NEW SCOTLAND YARD

SEA LIFE LONDON AQUARIUM

RD

YORK

BA

WESTMINSTER

COUNTY HALL

BELVEDERE

LONDON DUNGEON

ADDINGTON STREET

BRIDGE ST

WESTMINSTER BRIDGE

BIG BEN

FLORENCE NIGHTINGALE MUSEUM

HOUSES OF PARLIAMENT

VER

PALACE ROAD

UPPER MARS

ROYAL ST

4 Old Palace Yard

NT

ST THOMAS'

There are few surviving vestiges of this area's past; the swamps were drained centuries ago and the last war decimated the factories and workshops which, in the 19th century, had turned these villages into a vital industrial center. The land on the south bank of the river was subsequently cleared of rubble to build cultural facilities capable of rivaling those on the north bank. The Southbank Centre, created in 1951 for the Festival of Britain, was the first to rise to the challenge, followed by numerous others. Follow the Queen's Walk west to Westminster Bridge – it affords great views of the north bank across the river.

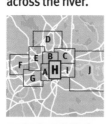

MESON DON FELIPE   **BALTIC**

RESTAURANTS

Meson
Don Felipe (D3) ¶❶¶
→ 53 The Cut, SE1
Tel. 020 7928 3237
Mon-Sat noon–11pm
A small, first-class Spanish tapas bar; the place is packed in the evening, with flamenco guitarists playing most nights. Very good wines. Tapas/entrées £5–11.

The Cut (D3) ¶❷¶
→ Young Vic, 66 The Cut, SE1; Tel. 020 7928 4400
Mon-Sat noon–11pm
Bar: Mon-Fri 8am (9am Sat)–last customer
Set within the Young Vic Theatre, and very much its match in laid-back inventiveness. A modern dining room and open-air terrace for simple organic dishes (fishcakes, burgers, risotto, salads or brunch. Entrées £7–14.

Masters
Super Fish (D4) ¶❸¶
→ 191 Waterloo Rd, SE1
Tel. 020 7928 6924; Mon-Sat noon–3pm, 4.30 (5.30pm Mon)–10.30pm (11pm Fri)
The decor of this fish & chip shop is nothing special, but the fresh fish (delivered daily from Billingsgate Market) is great and comes in huge portions. Well worth a

detour. Entrées £8–14.

Anchor & Hope
(D3) ¶❹¶
→ 36 The Cut, SE1
Tel. 020 7928 9898
Mon 5–11pm; Tue-Sat 11am–11pm; Sun 12.30–3pm (by reservation)
Popular gastropub on the South Bank. Frequently changing menu with dishes including grilled Orkney kipper with new potatoes; seven-hour lamb shoulder with gratin dauphinois; buttermilk pudding with peaches and raspberry sauce. Prix fixe (lunch) £15–17; entrées £8–35.

House
Restaurant (B2) ¶❺¶
→ National Theatre, South Bank, SE1
Tel. 020 7452 3600
Mon-Sat noon–2.30pm, 5–11pm; Sun noon–2.30pm
Enjoy a meal in the National Theatre's streamlined restaurant: pork medallions with spinach, baked sole, boeuf bourguignon. Entrées £14–21.

Baltic (D3) ¶❻¶
→ 74 Blackfriars Rd, SE1
Tel. 020 7928 1111; Daily noon–3pm, 5.30–11.15pm
This place has a long bar, a vast dining room with a glass roof supported by oak beams, a taste for

THE CUT THEATRES

KONDITOR & COOK

jazz music (live Sunday evenings) and great Polish food with some Mediterranean flavors: *golonka* (roast pork shank with sauerkraut and potato); Polish hunter's stew with venison. Good desserts, too. Entrées £18–20.

BARS, CAFÉ, PUB

Scooter Caffè (C4) **7**
➔ *132 Lower Marsh, SE1*
Tel. 020 7620 1421
Mon-Fri 8.30am–11pm (midnight Fri); Sat-Sun 10am–midnight (11pm Sun)
This cozy café with mismatching vintage furniture, set in a former Vespa garage, serves one of the best espressos this side of the Thames.

Fire Station (C3) **8**
➔ *150 Waterloo Rd, SE1*
Tel. 020 3727 5938; Mon-Fri 7am–11pm (midnight Thu-Fri); Sat-Sun 9am–midnight (10.30pm Sun)
Large, modern gastropub converted from a fire station. Excellent choice of draught beers and wines; wood-fired pizzas.

OXO Tower Bar (C2) **9**
➔ *OXO Tower Wharf, Barge House St, 8th floor, SE1; Tel. 020 7803 3888*
Mon-Sat 11am–11pm (midnight Fri-Sat);

Sun noon–10.30pm Brasserie: daily noon–11pm; Restaurant: daily noon–2.30pm, 6–11pm
The bar on the tower's eighth floor is worth a detour for the views of the Thames and the North Bank it affords. Live jazz nightly in the brasserie.

Cubana (C3) **10**
➔ *48 Lower Marsh, SE1*
Tel. 020 7928 8778
Mon-Fri noon–midnight (1am Wed-Thu, 3am Fri); Sat 1pm–3am; Sun 2–11pm
A quirky bar with religious trinkets, portraits of Che Guevara and photos of Cuba adorning the walls; and Latino music in the background. Cocktails, wine, beer and tapas; salsa Fri and Sat evening.

MOVIE THEATER, THEATER

BFI IMAX (C3) **11**
➔ *1 Charlie Chaplin Walk, SE1; Tel. 0330 333 7878*
bfi.org.uk/bfi-imax
The largest movie screen in the country.

The Cut Theatres
The Old Vic (C3) **12**
➔ *The Cut, SE1*
Tel. 0844 871 7628
oldvictheatre.com
Plush auditorium with a proscenium stage. Solid productions of

old and new plays, often featuring big names.

Young Vic (D3) **13**
➔ *66 The Cut, SE1*
Tel. 020 7922 2922
youngvic.org
New plays and innovative productions of classics.

SHOPPING

Konditor & Cook (C3) **14**
➔ *22 Cornwall Rd, SE1*
Tel. 020 7261 0456; Mon-Fri 7.30am–7pm; Sat 8.30am–6pm; Sun 11am–5pm
Behind Waterloo Station this patisserie is worth a detour for its fantastic range of cakes and buns, from humble scones to gorgeous gateaux.

What the Butler Wore (C4) **15**
➔ *108 Lower Marsh, SE1*
Tel. 020 7261 1968
Mon-Sat 11am–6pm
A small, second-hand clothes store for lovers of 1960s and 1970s styles. Everything is in excellent condition and, given the number of revivals, usually looks bang up-to-date.

Gramex (C3) **16**
➔ *104 Lower Marsh, SE1*
Tel. 020 7401 3830
Mon-Sat 11am–7pm
A key attraction for lovers of classical and jazz

music, some of whom come to sit and snooze in the comfy chairs at the back of the store. Vinyl, second-hand CDs and expert advice.

OXO Tower Design Shops (C2) **17**
➔ *OXO Tower Wharf, Barge House St, SE1*
Tue-Sun 11am–6pm
The restored Art Deco former power station houses shops and workshops belonging to independent designers; hand-woven silk, jewelry, children's clothes and small pieces of furniture.

Gabriel's Wharf (C2) **18**
➔ *56 Upper Ground, SE1*
Craft stores, boutiques, a children's play area – the little square and the few surrounding square yards would have ended up in the hands of a real estate developer (like the rest of the district) but was saved by the not-for-profit Coin Street Community Builders.

Ganesha
➔ *Daily 11.30am–7pm*
Cushions, tunics, bags and accessories in a boutique that celebrates Indian culture and craftsmanship while promoting fairtrade products.

SEX ST

MIDDLE TEMPLE LANE

THE TEMPLE

TUDOR STREET

TEMPLE GARDENS

J. CARPENTER ST

CARMELITE ST

QUEEN VICTORIA STREET

C | **D**

ACE

TEMPLE LANE

TEMPLE GARDENS

TEMPLE AVE

TALLIS ST

B

BLACKFRIARS STATION

1

VICTORIA EMBANKMENT

K I N G ' S   R E A C H

BLACKFRIARS BRIDGE ★

QUEEN'S WALK

OXO TOWER ★

WALK

GABRIEL'S WHARF

17 9

OXO TOWER WHARF

18

BARGE HOUSE ST

UPPER GROUND

UPPER GROUND

RENNIE STREET

BLACKFRIARS RD

HOPTON STREET

2

DUCHY

BROADWALL

COIN ST

STAMFORD ST

PARIS GDN

STREET

BURELL ST

BEAR LANE

NBANK

DON ST

CORNWALL ROAD

AQUINAS STREET

STAMFORD ST

HATFIELDS

B

COLOMBO ST

B

CHANCEL ST

B

NICHOLSON STREET

ST JOHN THE EVANGELIST

THEED ST

WHITTLESEY ST

SECKER ST

ME YMOTT ST

SCORESBY STREET

N WAY

EXTON ST

14

ROUPELL STREET

WATERLOO EAST STATION

HATFIELDS

B

B

SOUTHWARK

N APPROACH RD

SANDELL

WOOTTON

WINDMILL WALK

GREEN ST

B

UNION ST

STATION

8

CORNWALL

THE CUT

2 13

4

YOUNG VIC THEATRE

BURROWS MEWS

6

NELSON

SQUARE

3

THE CUT

SHORT ST

MITRE RD

1

STREET

BLACKFRIARS ROAD

SURREY ROW

THE OLD VIC

12

WEBBER STREET

UFFORD ST

CHAPLIN CLOSE

POCOCK ST

RUSHWORTH STREET

N APPROACH ROAD

SPUR ROAD

GRAY STREET

VALENTINE PLACE

BARON'S PLACE

10 B

16 B

WATERLOO ROAD

WEBBER ST

15

LOWER MARSH

CORAL STREET

3

WEBBER ROW

LANCASTER ST

B

MURPHY STREET

FRAZIER STREET

BAYLIS ROAD

EARMAN STREET

MORLEY STREET

GERRIDGE STREET

DODSON STREET

KING JAMES STREET

TH NORTH

GREENHAM CLOSE

St George's

BOROUGH ROAD

B

4

▲ Map C

SOUTHBANK CENTRE / HAYWARD GALLERY

LONDON EYE

▼ Map I

COUNTY HALL

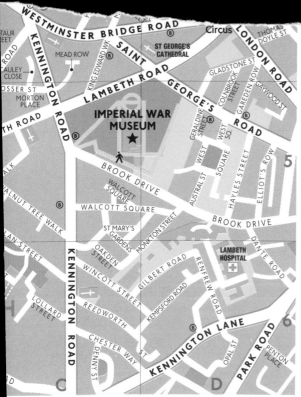

SEA LIFE LONDON AQUARIUM

IMPERIAL WAR MUSEUM

ankment to make
South Bank more
coming. Visitors,
ever, have always
ked to the concert
captivated by its vast,
-filled interior spaces.
during the day for a
lunchtime concert or in
evening for a drink at
Skylon Bar overlooking
illuminated riverside.
ward Gallery
or contemporary
ting, sculpture and
ography exhibitions
hown in this stark
s concrete gallery.
en Elizabeth Hall
e and classical music.
ell Room

A smaller hall for recitals
and chamber music.
→ *Restoration works are
being undertaken on the three
aforementioned spaces (due
to reopen end of 2017).*
Royal Festival Hall
A vast concert hall with
exceptional acoustics and
a varied program of jazz,
classical, rock and pop.
★ London Eye (B3)
→ *Queen's Walk, SE1*
Tel. 0871 781 3000
*Daily 10am–9pm (11.30pm
Fridays in summer)*
Take a 40-minute trip on
the tallest wheel in Europe.
From a height of 443 ft
you can enjoy (in good
weather) spectacular

views over London.
★ County Hall (B3)
→ *Riverside Building, Queen's
Walk; Tel. 020 7981 2550*
This impressive building
in Portland stone, with an
elegant Edwardian façade,
was designed by Ralph
Knott, and was the HQ of
the Greater London Council
(GLC) until 1986. Today, it
houses an aquarium,
restaurants and hotels.
★ London Dungeon (B3)
Tel. 0871 423 2240; *Daily
10am–5pm (6pm Sat-Sun)*
This ghoulish venue takes
you on an interactive tour
that recounts gruesome
events and crimes in
Britain's history.

**★ Sea Life London
Aquarium** (B3)
→ *Tel. 0871 663 1678
Daily 10am–7pm
(9am–8pm mid July-end Aug)*
Stroke the rays, watch the
sharks being fed and see
fish from all over the world.
**★ Imperial War
Museum** (C5)
→ *Lambeth Rd, SE1
Tel. 020 7416 5000
Daily 10am–6pm*
An unrivaled collection of
war memorabilia covering
the two World Wars, as
well as reconstructions
(including a trench from
World War One). There is
also a powerful exhibition
on the Holocaust.

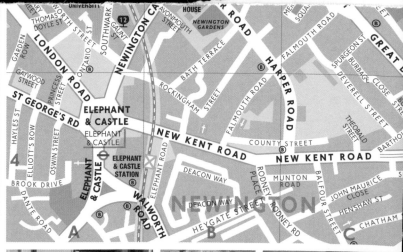

THE SHARD

SOUTHWARK CATHEDRAL

SHAKESPEARE'S GLOBE EXHIBITION

★ **Tower of London** (E1)
→ *Tower Hill, EC3*
Tel. 0844 482 7777
Daily 9am (10am Sun-Mon)–
5.30pm (4.30pm Nov-Feb)
William the Conqueror
built the tower to ensure
control of the river. The
impregnable fortress was
also used as a jail, and
famous prisoners have
included Anne Boleyn, Guy
Fawkes and Rudolf Hess.
The Yeomen Warders, in
Tudor costume, continue
to mount guard and the
Crown Jewels, used for
coronations, are on show.

★ **Tower Bridge** (F1)
→ *Daily 10am–5.30pm*
(9.30am–5pm in winter)

The distinctive silhouette
of Tower Bridge evokes the
Victorian era when England
was a powerful seafaring
nation. River traffic was
then extremely heavy and
the movable bridges were
raised to allow ships to
pass through. The two
neo-Gothic towers
conceal the complex
hydraulic lifting machinery
used to raise the two
1,000-ton bascules. Within,
the Tower Bridge Exhibition
recounts the bridge's
history. There are great
views from the spectacular
glass floor that forms part
of the high-level walkway,
42m above the water.

★ **City Hall** (E2)
→ *Queen's Walk, SE1*
Tel. 020 7983 4000; Mon-Fri
8am–6pm (5.30pm Fri)
London's City Hall, in the
unusual shape of a sloping
cone with a glass façade,
was designed by architect
Norman Foster (2002).
Inside, a 1,640-ft helical
walkway ascends the full
height of the building.

★ **Fashion and Textile
Museum** (D2)
→ *83 Bermondsey St, SE1*
Tel. 020 7407 8664
Tue-Sun 11am–6pm
(8pm Thu, 5pm Sun)
This museum was founded
in 2008 by the designer
Zandra Rhodes in a two-

toned building designed
by the Mexican architect
Ricardo Legorreta (2001)
Textiles, clothes, shoes
and jewelry by top name
such as Marian Clayden
and Alexander McQueen
as well as lesser known
talents.

★ **HMS Belfast** (D1)
→ *Queen's Walk, SE1*
Daily 10am–6pm (5pm win
Experience the life of a
sailor onboard a warship
This one was in service
from 1938 to the end of
the Korean War in 1953.

★ **The Shard** (D2)
→ *32 London Bridge St, SE*
Tel. 0844 499 7111
Daily 10am–10pm (7pm

TOWER OF LONDON

TOWER BRIDGE

CITY HALL

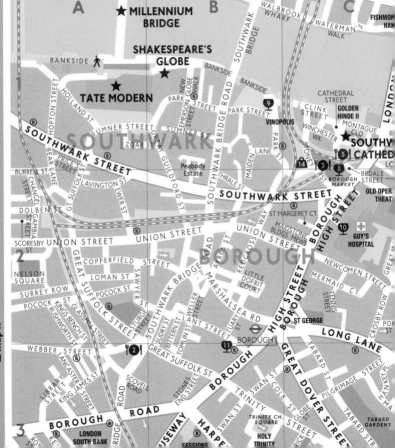

▲ Map H

★ MILLENNIUM BRIDGE

★ SHAKESPEARE'S GLOBE

★ TATE MODERN

BANKSIDE

WALBROOK WHARF

WATERMAN'S WALK

FISHMON HA

A   B   C

SOUTHWARK BRIDGE

BANKSIDE

BANKSIDE

NEW GLOBE WALK

EMERSON STREET

PARK STREET

PARK STREET

SOUTHWARK BRIDGE ROAD

CATHEDRAL STREET

CLINK STREET

GOLDEN HINDE II

9 VINOPOLIS

MONTAGUE CLO.

WINCHESTER WK

HOPTON STREET

HOLLAND ST

SUMNER STREET

GREAT GUILDFORD ST

ZOAR ST

SUMNER ST

SOUTHWARK

SOUTHWARK STREET

BEAR LANE

PRICE ST

SUFFOLK ST

BURRELL ST

CHANCEL SAMBIA STREET

LAVINGTON ST

EWER ST

Peabody Estate

THRALE ST

MAIDEN LANE

STONEY

PARK ST

14   3   8

BOROUGH MARKET

SOUTHW CATHED

5   LC

BEDALE STREET

OLD OPER THEAT

DOLBEN ST

SAMBIA STREET

SCORESBY ST

UNION STREET

ST MARGERET CT.

MAIDSTONE BLDGS MEWS

UNION STREET

BOROUGH HIGH STREET

10 GUY'S HOSPITAL

GREAT M

UNION STREET

UNION STREET

WAY

REDCROSS WAY

BOROUGH

NELSON SQUARE

COPPERFIELD STREET

LOMAN ST

SAWYER ST

ACRES ST

LITTLE DOFRIT COURT

NEWCOMEN STREET

MERMAID CT.

SURREY ROW

POCOCK ST

GREAT SUFFOLK STREET

KINGS BENCH ST

GLASSHILL STREET

RUSHWORTH ST

STURGE ST

SOUTHWARK BRIDGE ROAD

MARSHALSEA RD

TENNIS STREET

CROSBY ROW

POO ST

POCOCK ST

2

WEBBER STREET

LANCASTER

SUDREY ST

BITTERN ST

TOMLIN ST

WELLER STREET

TUARY ST

ST GEORGE

LONG LANE

TABARD STREET

PILGRIMAGE STREET

HA

LIBRARY STREET

KING JAMES STREET

SCOVELL ROAD

GREAT SUFFOLK ST

STONES END STREET

BOROUGH

11

BOROUGH

GREAT DOVER STREET

TABARD GARDENS

3

BOROUGH

LONDON SOUTH BANK

BRIDGE

ROAD

USEWAY

HARPER

SESSIONS

SWAN ST

COLE

TRINITY

SWAN ST

TRINITY CH. SQUARE

GLOBE

STREET

HOLY TRINITY

2

Historically a downtrodden area abounding in brothels, taverns and theaters, Southwark went on to enjoy prosperity through maritime trade but the closure of its docks in the 1970s triggered another decline. It has now experienced a comeback as a showcase for cutting-edge architecture, as with Tate Modern, City Hall and the Shard (the tallest building in the country). Fashionable restaurants and cafés flourish around Borough Market, while the warehouses on Bermondsey Street have been converted into loft apartments. Along the banks of the Thames, the refurbished Queen's Walk runs past luxury homes to connect Tower Bridge with the London Eye.

M. MANZE

EL VERGEL

RESTAURANTS

M. Manze (D3) ⑪❶⑪
→ 87 Tower Bridge Rd, SE1
Mon-Thu 10.30am (11am Mon)–2pm; Fri-Sat 10am–2.30pm (3pm Sat)
The traditional dish of 'pie & mash with eels' is rarely found on a menu nowadays. Take out or eat in the family-run 100-year-old canteen-like restaurant. Vegetarian pies too. £3–6.

El Vergel (A3) ⑪❷⑪
→ 132 Webber St, SE1
Tel. 020 7401 2308; Mon-Fri 8am–3pm; Sat 10am–4pm
A successful Latin-American eatery, five minutes from Borough subway station. Tacos, empanadas, Chilean steaks and first-class service. Entrées £4–8.

Borough Market (C2) ⑪❸⑪
→ 8 Southwark St, SE1
Mon-Tue 10am–5pm (only the restaurants within the market space); Wed-Fri 10am–5pm (6pm Fri); Sat 8am–5pm
This wonderful outdoor market, whose present buildings were designed in 1851, offers the finest organic and farm-produced goods. Ready-to-eat foods on offer for lunch: delicious pies, barbecued meats, bagels... From £5.

Maria's Market Café
→ Borough Market, Stoney St, SE1
Wed-Sat 5am–2.30pm (4pm Thu-Fri, 5pm Sat)
If your heart is set on a traditional English breakfast, this café, deep in the heart of Borough, is one of the best. Not exactly fat-free but there are lighter alternatives.

Maltby Street Market (E3) ⑪❹⑪
→ Maltby St, SE1; Sat-Sun 9am (11am Sun)–4pm
An array of quality food stands, pop-up bars and eateries of all kinds: fresh waffles, cured and cold-smoked salmon, Brazilian dishes, handmade chocolate truffles, fruit gins... From £5.

Fish! (C1) ⑪❺⑪
→ Cathedral St, SE1
Tel. 020 7407 3803
Mon-Fri 11.30am (11am Fri)–11pm; Sat-Sun 10am–11pm (10.30pm Sun)
A steel and glass structure serving dishes depending on the daily deliveries: squid, cod, swordfish, skate. Also serves breakfast and brunch. Entrées £13–30.

Tanner & Co (D2) ⑪❻⑪
→ 50 Bermondsey St, SE1
Tel. 020 7357 0244

STONE ARMS

BOROUGH MARKET

BERMONDSEY SQUARE MARKET

Mon–Thu noon–5pm;
Fri noon–3pm, 7–10pm
A light, airy spot offering
dishes and finger food
based on traditional
British fare, with a
modern twist: chicken
liver mousse with
madeira jelly, potted
rabbit, black pudding;
also steaks, fish, pies,
etc. Entrées £14–20.

Butlers Wharf Chop House (F2) 🍴🎧
→ 36 Shad Thames, Butlers
Wharf; Tel. 020 7403 3403
Bar: daily noon–11pm
(10pm Sun); Restaurant:
daily noon–4pm, 6–11pm
(10pm Sun)
This restaurant near
Tower Bridge, created
by the designer Terence
Conran serves resolutely
British fare on traditional
white tablecloths:
steamed Shetland
mussels, roast Yorkshire
lamb with mint and
redcurrant jellies, lemon
curd with shortbread.
Entrées £14–28.

WINE BAR, PUBS, CLUB

Bedales Wines (C1) 🔟8
→ Borough Market, Bedale
St; Tel. 020 7403 8853
Mon-Sat 10am (9.30am Sat)
–11pm; Sun 12.30–9pm
A store that stocks wines

from all over the world,
with a small bar where
customers can sample
them – alongside cheese,
cooked meats and tapas.
Live music at various
times.

The Anchor (B1) 🟡9
→ 34 Park St, Bankside, SE1
Mon-Fri 11am–midnight;
Sat-Sun noon–11pm
A historic pub, originally
built in 1676. In summer,
its terrace is a perfect
spot to enjoy a drink in
the sunshine.

George Inn (C2) 🟡10
→ 75-77 Borough High St,
SE1; Mon-Sat 11am–11pm;
Sun noon-10.30pm
This listed building dating
from 1676 is London's
only surviving galleried
coaching inn. There is a
restaurant upstairs in the
former bedrooms and
some small rooms at
street level that can only
be accessed from the
pretty cobbled courtyard.

Gladstone Arms (B3) 🟡11
→ 64 Lant St, SE1
Mon-Fri noon–11pm
(midnight Fri); Sat-Sun 1pm
–midnight (10.30pm Sun)
A real local pub, relaxed
and unpretentious, set on
two floors. At street level
there's live music and DJ
sessions, while upstairs
a cozy bar provides a

place to chat and play
pub games; beers,
ciders and great pies.

Ministry of Sound (A3) 🟡12
→ 103 Gaunt St, SE1
Fri 10.30pm–6am;
Sat 11pm–7am
ministryofsound.com
More than a nightclub –
a brand and a legend –
with an exceptional
sound system. Three
dance floors play techno,
garage, RnB and house.

ART GALLERY

White Cube (D3) 🟥13
→ 144-152 Bermondsey St,
SE1; Tel. 020 7930 5373; Tue-
Sun 10am (noon Sun)–6pm
Jay Jopling's third gallery,
housed in a 1970s
warehouse – an immense
space measuring over
50,000 sq. ft. Like its two
sister galleries, it is a key
venue for contemporary
international and British
artists (including Damien
Hirst and Tracey Emin).
Has an ongoing series of
artist films and lectures in
the purpose-built
auditorium.

SHOPPING

Neal's Yard Dairy (C1) 🟥14
→ 6 Park St, SE1

Tel. 020 7367 0799; Mon-Sat
9am (8am Sat)–6pm
Shelves from floor to
ceiling stacked with
maturing wheels of
farmhouse cheeses.

Hay's Galleria (D1) 🟥15
→ Hay's Wharf,
Counter St, SE1
Two impressive 19th-
century red-brick and
light stone buildings once
used as warehouses for
storing butter and spices,
are connected by a
passageway with a glazed
barrel vault supported
by a slender steel
framework. Inside: cafés,
restaurants and stores.

Le Pont de la Tour Food Store (F2) 🟥16
→ 36D Shad Thames,
Butlers Wharf, SE1
Mon-Fri 7.30am–8pm;
Sat-Sun 9am–6pm
A gourmet deli which also
sells great sandwiches.

Bermondsey Square Market (E3) 🟥17
→ Bermondsey Square, SE1
Fri-Sat 6am (10am Sat)–
2pm
The Friday antiques
market is frequented by
many dealers – proof that
there are bargains to be
had if you're an early
riser. On Saturdays,
antiques give way to
stalls of fresh food from
British farms.

HMS BELFAST

FASHION AND TEXTILE MUSEUM

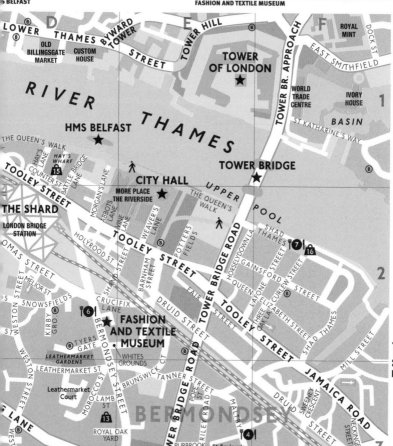

▲ Map C

LOWER THAMES STREET

D

BYWARD TOWER

E

TOWER HILL

F

ROYAL MINT

DOCK ST.

OLD BILLINGSGATE MARKET

CUSTOM HOUSE

TOWER OF LONDON ★

TOWER BR. APPROACH

EAST SMITHFIELD

WORLD TRADE CENTRE

IVORY HOUSE

1

RIVER

THAMES

St KATHARINE'S WAY

BASIN

HMS BELFAST ★

THE QUEEN'S WALK

HAY'S LANE

HAY'S WHARF

COUNTER ST.

BATTLE BRIDGE LANE

15

TOOLEY STREET

THE SHARD

LONDON BRIDGE STATION

MORGAN'S LANE

ABBOTS LANE

VINE LANE

WEAVER'S LANE

MORE PLACE THE RIVERSIDE ★

CITY HALL

THE QUEEN'S WALK

TOWER BRIDGE ★

UPPER POOL

SHAD THAMES

7 16

HOLYROOD ST

TOOLEY STREET

POTTERS FIELDS

TOWER BRIDGE ROAD

HORSELYDOWN LA.

GAINSFORD STREET

LAFONE STREET

QUEEN ELIZABETH STREET

OAK LA.

CURLEW STREET

SHAD THAMES

THOMAS STREET

MELIOR ST

BARNHAM STREET

SHAD STREET

DRUID STREET

FAIR STREET

TOOLEY STREET

THREE OAK LA.

SNOWSFIELDS

CRUCIFIX LANE

6

KIRBY GRO.

TYERS GATE

FASHION AND TEXTILE MUSEUM ★

BERMONDSEY STREET

WHITES GROUNDS

2

WESTON STREET

LEATHERMARKET GARDENS

LEATHERMARKET ST

Leathermarket Court

MOROCCO ST

LAMB ST

BRUNSWICK CT.

TANNER STREET

POPE ST

RILEY ROAD

MALTBY ST

JAMAICA ROAD

DRUID STREET

MILL STREET

SWEENEY CRESCENT

NECKINGER STREET

LANE

WESTON STREET

13

ROYAL OAK YARD

BERMONDSEY SQUARE

LONG

TOWER BRIDGE ROAD

PURBROOK STREET

St Saviour's Estate

4

BERMONDSEY

3

▼ Map J

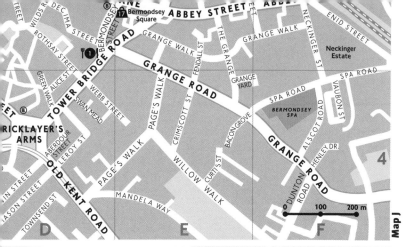

Map J

...MODERN

MILLENNIUM BRIDGE

...rtain days in winter)
...o Piano's glass-clad
...craper, at over 1,000
...s redefined London's
...ne. The pyramidal
...r has 72 habitable
...s, with a viewing
...ry and open-air
...rvation deck (the UK's
...est) on the 72nd floor,
...eight of 804 ft.

...outhwark
...edral (C1)
...ndon Bridge, SE1; Daily
...8.30am Sat-Sun)–6pm
...of the few
...ges of the district's
...eval past, William
...espeare's brother
...und is buried here.
...hurch has been

remodeled on many
occasions but the current
building retains the choir
and the ambulatory of the
Gothic church (1273). The
triforium was inspired by
the cathedrals of Chartres
and Reims in France.
Wenceslaus Hollar painted
his famous *Long View Of
London* (1647) from the top
of the towers.

★ Shakespeare's
Globe (B1)
→ *New Globe Walk, SE1*
Tel. 020 7902 1400
Guided tours (every 30 mins):
daily 9.30am–5pm. For
exhibition opening times go
to: shakespearesglobe.com
Visit the reconstruction

of Shakespeare's Globe
(1599) theater and the
museum charting its epic
construction. It was built
close to the original site,
using 17th-century
materials and methods.
★ Tate Modern (A1)
→ *Bankside, SE1*
Tel. 020 7887 8888; Daily
10am–6pm (10pm Fri-Sat)
In 2000 Herzog and de
Meuron completed their
spectacular museum of
international modern art
in the old Bankside power
station, including the
Boiler House and the
115-ft-high Turbine Hall. In
2016 the same architects
opened a futuristic 10-story

extension (Switch House)
with a roof terrace. Its new
galleries present some of
the permanent collection
(Manet's *Nymphs*, Bacon's
tryptichs) and play host to
performances, installations
and contemporary
photography.
★ Millennium
Bridge (A1)
→ *Across from Tate Modern*
The steel and aluminium
foot suspension bridge
(2000), the first bridge to
be built in London for over
a century, was designed
by Foster + Partners in
collaboration with sculptor
Anthony Caro. It links the
South Bank with St Paul's.

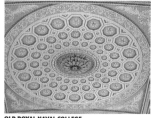
OLD ROYAL NAVAL COLLEGE

THE QUEEN'S HOUSE

NATIONAL MARITIME MUSE

★ Whitechapel Art Gallery (A2)

→ *77-82 Whitechapel High St, E1; Tel. 020 7522 7888; Tue-Sun 11am–6pm (9pm Thu)*
The gallery, founded in 1901 to bring 'great art to the people of east London', was the one to premiere in the UK the likes of Frida Kahlo, Jackson Pollock and Mark Rothko. It continues to showcase major contemporary artists.

★ V&A Museum of Childhood (B1)

→ *Cambridge Heath Rd, E2 Tel. 020 8983 5200 Daily 10am–5.45pm*
A glorious jumble of a museum: rocking horses, Punch and Judy, airplanes and dolls' houses from the 17th to the 21st centuries.

★ Museum of London Docklands (D2)

→ *No.1 Warehouse, West India Quay, E14; Tel. 020 7001 9844; Daily 10am–6pm*
This disused 18th-century warehouse was converted into a museum exploring the fascinating history of the Port of London: Roman and Viking remains, model ships, a reconstructed Victorian street etc.

★ Canary Wharf (D2)

By the late 1980s the London Docks were nearing the end of their active life and developers began acquiring the area. The extension of the Jubilee Line (1993) enabled large City companies to move here, to a maze of streets and underground walkways at the foot of skyscrapers. At the exit of the subway station (Norman Foster, 1999) is One Canada Square, Cesar Pelli's 771-ft stainless-steel covered tower (1991).

★ Greenwich Foot Tunnel (D4)

→ *Daily 24h/24*
In 1902, this 400-yard-long tunnel 50 ft under the Thames replaced the ferries that transported the dockers working on the South Bank to and fro. entrances are indicate two traffic circles, one the Isle of Dogs, the ot by Greenwich Pier.

★ Cutty Sark (D4)

→ *King William Walk, SE1 Daily 10am–5pm*
Built in 1869, this famo ship is the last survivin tea clipper. Visitors can walk the decks, explore its rich history and even venture directly underneath to view the sleek lines of its hull.

★ Old Royal Naval College (E4)

→ *SE10; Tel. 020 8269 47 Painted Hall and Chapel (free): daily 10am–5pm*

WHITECHAPEL ART GALLERY

V&A MUSEUM OF CHILDHOOD

MUSEUM OF LONDON DOCKLANDS

On either side of the Thames rises London's celebrated East End. On the south side, buoyed up by the success of Canary Wharf, the enclave of futuristic skyscrapers, are the former docks with their rows of converted warehouses. From the Isle of Dogs, once home to the kennels of King Henry VIII, the Thames can be crossed on foot to reach the old town of Greenwich, whose park is bisected by the Meridian Line. On the north side, around Spitalfields and the former working-class district of Bethnal Green, vintage shops and fashionable bars vie for space with the street markets and curry houses of Brick Lane.

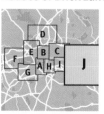

RIVINGTON GRILL GREENWICH

BRAWN

RESTAURANTS

E. Pellicci (B4) 🍴◐
→ *332 Bethnal Green Rd, E2*
Tel. 020 7739 4873
Mon-Sat 7am–4.30pm
Family-run for three generations, this Italian restaurant offers home cooking in a small dining room. Hearty English breakfasts, pasta, steak and fries. Entrées £7–9.

Tayyabs (B1) 🍴❷
→ *83-89 Fieldgate St, E1*
Tel. 020 7247 9543
Daily noon–11.30pm
Opened in 1972, this family-owned-and-run curry restaurant is one of the oldest in London. Reserve. Entrées £7–13.

Rivington Grill Greenwich (D4) 🍴❸
→ *178 Greenwich High Road*
Tel. 020 8293 9270
Daily noon (10am Sat-Sun)–10pm (11pm Fri)
The best of British cuisine in a seasonal menu: fish & chips with mushy peas, sausages with mash. Breakfast at weekends. Entrées £11–25.

Brawn (A3) 🍴❹
→ *49 Columbia Rd, E2*
Tel. 020 7729 5692; Mon 6–11pm; Tue-Sat noon–3pm, 6–11pm; Sun noon–4pm
With white-washed brick walls, mismatched tables and chairs, Brawn prides itself on a seasonal menu using locally sourced produce. Mediterranean-inspired menu, with an 'all things pork' section. Prix fixe (Sun only) £28; entrées £13–19.

The Gun (E2) 🍴❺
→ *27 Coldharbour, E14*
Tel. 020 7515 5222; Daily 11am–midnight (11pm Sun); kitchen closes 3–6pm
A historic inn, where Horatio Nelson used to meet Emma Hamilton. It has a terrace overlooking the river, three bars and a gastro-dining area. Entrées £15–26.

Café Spice Namasté (A2) 🍴❻
→ *16 Prescot St, E1*
Tel. 020 7488 9242; Mon-Fri noon–3pm, 6.15–10.30pm; Sat 6.30–10.30pm
Superb cuisine from Goa in a Gothic-inspired setting reinterpreted à la Bollywood! Try the slow-cooked shank of pork in Goan *Balchao* masala. Entrées £17.

CAFÉS, PUBS

Pavilion Café (E4) 🍷
→ *Greenwich Park, Blackheath Ave, SE10*
Daily 9am–4pm/5pm/6pm according to the season
After the stiff climb up to the observatory, relax on

COLUMBIA ROAD MARKET

MUDCHUTE CITY FARM

ET EAST

the terrace or in the small octagonal pavilion for a sandwich or a scone.

The Mayflower (B3) ⑧
→ 117 Rotherhithe St , SE16
Tel. 020 7237 4088
Daily 11am–11pm
With a terrace overlooking the river, this is the oldest pub along the Thames (1621), sited in what was once the ancient village of Rotherhithe.

Dickens Inn (A2) ⑨
→ St Katharine's Way, E1
Tel. 020 7488 2208
Daily 11am–midnight (10.30pm Sun–Mon)
A huge three-story, pseudo-Swiss chalet with fantastic views over the river and Tower Bridge from its broad balconies.

Greenwich Union (D4) ⑩
→ 56 Royal Hill, SE1
Tel. 020 8692 6258; Mon–Fri noon–11pm; Sat–Sun 10am–11pm (10.30pm Sun)
With a leafy courtyard extending behind pretty cottage premises, this is a relaxed pub with music.

CULTURAL CENTER, MUSIC VENUE, CLUB

Rich Mix (A4) ⑪
→ 35-47 Bethnal Green Rd, E1; Tel. 020 7613 7498

Mon–Fri 9am–10pm (1am depending on the event); Sat–Sun 10pm–1am
This independent cultural center set in a former garment factory is a hive of contemporary creativity: arthouse cinema, theater, dance, exhibitions, concerts.

93 Feet East (A4) ⑫
→ 150 Brick Lane, E2
Tel. 020 7770 6006
Tue-Sat 5–11pm (1am Fri-Sat); Sun 3–10.30pm
Graffiti-covered walls in this music venue which hosts electro nights as well as good rock gigs.

Bethnal Green Working Men's Club (B3) ⑬
→ 42-44 Pollard Row, E2
Tel. 020 7739 7170
workersplaytime.net
Opened in 1953 as a place for workers to come and unwind, this club, cultural venue and party house stages all kinds of live, outlandish entertainment events.

SHOPPING

Cheshire Street (B4) ⑭
For vintage and unique fashion and craft stores.
The Shop (no. 3)
→ Mon-Sat 11am–6pm; Sun 9.30am–5pm

A little vintage shop piled from floor to ceiling with fabrics and textiles, hats, scarves, aprons, tablecloths, etc.
Cock & Bull & Co. (no. 30)
→ Daily noon–6pm
Sustainable and ethical menswear boutique: tweed waistcoats, hemp jeans, stylish knitwear in organic, recycled and locally sourced fabrics.

The Laden Showroom (A4) ⑮
→ 103 Brick Lane, E1
Tel. 020 7247 2431; Mon-Sat 11am–6.30pm (7pm Sat); Sun 10.30am–6pm
Women's fashion store supporting and selling the work of young designers. Original styles at affordable prices.

Son of a Stag (A4) ⑯
→ Old Truman Brewery, 91 Brick Lane, E2; Tel. 020 7247 3333; Mon-Sat 10.30am–7pm (7.30pm Wed, Fri; 8pm Thu); Sun 11.15am–6pm
A denim store specializing in hard-to-find labels. Also exclusive footwear brands such as Wolverine 1000 Miles.

Brick Lane Market (A4) ⑰
→ Brick Lane and Old Truman Brewery; Stands: Sunday 11am–5pm
This time-honored

flea market has become one of London's most fashionable commercial hubs, with stores, restaurants and galleries surrounding the stalls selling old books, vintage clothing, etc. Street food from around the world.

Columbia Road Flower Market (A3) ⑱
→ Sun 8am–3pm
Charming flower market on a street lined with independent boutiques and cafés.

Billingsgate Market (D2) ⑲
→ Trafalgar Way, E14
Tue-Sat 4–8am
On the Isle of Dogs near Canary Wharf, London's central fish market is at its busiest before most of the city's workers are out of bed in the morning.

ECOTOURISM

Mudchute City Farm (D3) ⑳
→ Pier St, Isle of Dogs, E14
Tel. 020 7515 590
Daily 8am–5pm; park open sunrise to sunset
Set in 32 acres of countryside in the heart of East London, the Mudchute is a community charity, with a working farm, stables and a children's nursery.

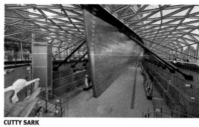

ARY WHARF

CUTTY SARK

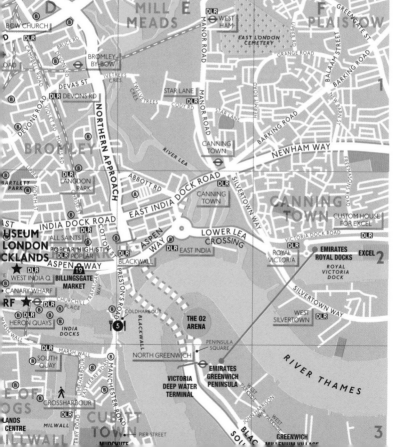

OLD ROYAL OBSERVATORY

RANGER'S HOUSE

nds: 8am–6pm
uperb collection of
buildings comprising
aval College include
aroque masterpieces
en on the south side.
ne Painted Hall is
ed in trompe-l'oeil
s by Thornhill. Facing
nds the chapel of St
and St Paul, richly
rated by James
nian' Stuart. The
ver Greenwich Visitor
e tells the story of
eople who shaped
wich.

e Queen's
e (E4)

nney Road, SE10
o 8312 6693

Daily 10am–5pm
The first classical structure
to be built in England, this
Palladian villa (Inigo Jones,
1616) made a formal
break with the traditions of
Elizabethan extravagance.
Inside are historic royal
portraits, a view of
Greenwich by Canaletto,
works by Hogarth and
Gainsborough, and a
superb black-and-white
tiled floor in the Great Hall.

★ National
Maritime Museum (E4)
→ *Park Row, SE10; Tel. 020*
8858 4422; Daily 10am–5pm
A magnificent naval
museum explaining the
conquest of the Empire, life

on board the great liners,
polar exploration and more
(including the jacket, with
bullet hole, that Admiral
Nelson was wearing when
he died at the Battle of
Trafalgar).

★ Old Royal
Observatory (E4)
→ *Greenwich Park, SE10*
Tel. 020 8858 4422
Daily 10am–5pm
On the orders of King
Charles II in 1675, Wren
built an observatory in
Greenwich Park to 'perfect
the art of navigation'. In the
oldest building, Flamsteed
House, is the Octagon
Room designed by Wren,
while the Meridian

Building houses a
collection of astronomical
instruments. In the north
courtyard, a line represents
the official Greenwich
Meridian.

★ Ranger's House (E4)
→ *Chesterfield Walk, SE10*
Tel. 020 8853 0035
Guided tours by reservation
(see website)
This red-brick Georgian
mansion (1723) houses
the collection of diamond
magnate Julius Wernher
(1850–1912): ivory, jewelry,
bronzes and porcelain.
Also paintings by Filippino
Lippi, Memling, De Hooch,
Romney, Reynolds and
many others.

AIRPORT LINKS

From Heathrow
Subway
→ *Piccadilly line; 1hr to city center; £5.70*
Heathrow Express (train)
→ *To Paddington Station* (**F** F1)*; 15 mins; £22 one way*

From Gatwick
Gatwick Express (train)
→ *To Victoria Station* (**A** A4) *30 mins; £19.90 one way*

From Stansted
Stansted Express (train)
→ *To Liverpool St Station* (**C** E3)*; 45 mins; £19 one way*

EasyBus
→ *From Gatwick, Stansted and London Luton airports to city center; 30 mins–1 hr/25 mins; £1.95–8.95*

'ROUTEMASTER' BUS

THE UNDERGROUND (SUBWAY)

SANTANDER CYCLES

VIA THE CHANNEL

Eurostar train
From Paris (2 hr 15 mins), Brussels (2 hrs), Lille (1 hr 10 mins) or Calais (1 hr). You arrive at St Pancras International (**D** D3), in central London.
Information/Reservation
→ *Tel. 03432 186 186 (UK); 01233 617 575 (outside UK)* From £69 / €84 return; *eurostar.com*
From the USA
→ *Tel. 1 877 677 1066 britrail.com*
→ *Tel. 1 877 257 2887 raileurope.com/us*

Eurotunnel
Calais-Folkestone
→ *Up to four departures/hr, 24/7 (boarding time 30 mins; journey time 35 mins)*
Travel by car via the Channel Tunnel (you stay with your vehicle throughout the journey).
→ *Tel. 08443 35 35 35 (UK); 08 10 63 03 04 (France); eurotunnel.com*

Boats
For passengers and vehicules. Price depends on length of stay.
DFDS Seaways
→ *dfdsseaways.co.uk*
Dunkirk to Dover
P&O Ferries
→ *poferries.com*
Calais to Dover.

BIKES

Santander Cycles
→ *tfl.gov.uk/modes/cycling/santander-cycles*
Network of self- service bikes (see 'B' symbols on map pages)
→ *Access fee: £2/24hrs Useage: free for first 30 mins then £2 for each additional 30 mins; payable by credit card*

Lancaster Hall Hotel (**F** E2)
→ *35 Craven Terrace, W2* Tel. 020 7723 9276 *lancaster-hall-hotel.co.uk*
Interesting for the 22 rooms in its youth wing (which are not only for young people!). Simply furnished (single, twin, triple and quadruple rooms) with shared bathrooms. £57.

Oakley Hotel (**G** C4)
→ *73 Oakley St, SW3* Tel. 020 7352 5599 *oakleyhotel.com*
A traditional 13-room B&B, well situated by Albert Bridge and close to the King's Road. £90–110.

Cherry Court Hotel (**A** A5)
→ *23 Hugh St, SW1* Tel. 020 7828 2840 *cherrycourthotel.co.uk*
A B&B in a five-story Victorian house, with 12 small but tasteful rooms. A basic breakfast is served

in the rooms. £75.

Portobello Gold (**F** B2)
→ *95-97 Portobello Rd, W11* Tel. 020 7460 4910 *portobellogold.com*
Set above a bar-restaurant with a glass atrium, the simple rooms here have been recently renovated. There is a honeymoon suite with a four-poster bed, and a rooftop apartment (sleeps up to six) whose roof terrace was featured in the movie *Notting Hill*. Note: the neighborhood is not the quietest. £80–115.

A Better Way to Stay (off map **F** A4)
→ *31 Rowan Rd, W6* Tel. 020 8748 0930 *abetterwaytostay.co.uk*
Two studios and two bedrooms that justify a detour off the beaten track. Home comforts, good taste and tranquility. £90–130 (min. two nights or £20 supplement).

Jesmond Dene Hotel (**D** D3)
→ *27 Argyle St, WC1* Tel. 020 7837 4654 *jesmonddenehotel.co.uk*
Well-cared for and elegant rooms. Two-minute walk from King's Cross St Pancras subway station. £90–180.

£100–150

The Hoxton Hotel (**C** E1)
→ *81 Great Eastern St, EC2* Tel. 020 7550 1000 *thehoxton.com*
Unique concept for a hotel in keeping with its hip Shoreditch surroundings. Modern, super comfy rooms with flat screen TVs, free Wifi, free local phone calls, luxurious duvets and rainmaker showers. And a daily breakfast bag delivered to your room. Restaurant downstairs. £100 (if booked at least one month ahead)–330.

AIRPORTS

Heathrow and Gatwick are the two largest of London's five international airports. Low-cost airlines mainly fly from Stansted and Luton.

Heathrow Airport
→ Tel. 0844 335 1801
heathrow.com

Gatwick Airport
→ Tel. 0844 892 0322
gatwickairport.com

Stansted Airport
→ Tel. 0844 335 1803
stanstedairport.com

City Airport
→ Tel. 020 7646 0088
londoncityairport.com

London Luton Airport
→ Tel. 01582 405100
london-luton.co.uk

AIRPORTS

Finding a clean, comfortable and reasonably priced hotel in London is a challenge. Hotels in the UK's capital city can be, given their high prices, less comfortable than those in other European capitals. Unless otherwise indicated, the prices listed here are per night for a double room en suite, VAT and breakfast included in mid season. Most hotels offer free Wifi access.

HOUSE/ APARTMENT RENTAL

One Fine Stay
→ Tel. 020 3588 0600
onefinestay.com
Stay in someone's stylish, characterful home while they're out of town. Beautifully decorated and equipped with all the latest amenities and home-from-home luxuries; range of rates to suit different budgets.

Airbnb
→ airbnb.com
Accommodation to rent in private owners' homes: from individual rooms to whole apartments or houses. All around the city with budgets to suit all.

BED & BREAKFAST

The Bed & Breakfast Club
→ thebedandbreakfastclub.co.uk
Stylish bed and breakfast accommodation in hand-picked private homes situated around London (both central and in more suburban areas); around £100 with breakfast.

YOUTH HOSTELS

Generator (D D4)
→ Compton Place, off 37 Tavistock Place, WC1
Tel. 020 7388 7666
generatorhostels.com

This private youth hostel is housed in an old police station and has a good central location. Modern decor, cinema, bar and nightly events. Dorms (3–12 beds) from £11–17/pers; double rooms from £55 (shared bathrooms).

Smart Camden Inn (D C3)
→ 55-57 Bayham St, NW1
Tel. 020 7388 8900
This backpackers' hostel is well equipped and friendly. Dorms (4–14 beds) from £12–21/pers; double rooms £50.

London YHA
→ yha.org.uk
The Youth Hostel Association's network of hostels. You must become a member (online or at the hostel on arrival: £20; £10 if under 26 years old). Dormitory beds from £15–21.

London St Pauls (C B3)
→ 36 Carter Lane, EC4
Tel. 0845 371 9012

London St Pancras (D D3)
→ 79-81 Euston Rd, NW1
Tel. 0845 371 9344

London Thameside (J C2)
→ 20 Salter Rd, SE16.
Tel. 0845 371 9756

London Oxford Street (B B3)
→ 14 Noel St, W1
Tel. 0845 371 9133

London Earl's Court (G A3)
→ 38 Bolton Gardens, SW5
Tel. 0845 371 9114

London Central (E D3)
→ 104 Bolsover St, W1
Tel. 0845 371 9154

UNDER £100

Marble Arch Inn (E B4)
→ 49-50 Upper Berkeley St, W1; Tel. 020 7723 7888
marblearch-inn.co.uk
One of the cheapest hotels to be found in the city, not far from Hyde Park; comfortable rooms. From £39 (no breakast).

Best of the best

10 must-have experiences to seek out when in London

Dress vintage

When it's a question of what to wear and seeking out a bargain, young Londoners like to buy famous brands second-hand. There are plenty of flea markets and vintage and retro shops, but the best bargains come from charity shops – especially those lining the streets of such well-heeled areas as South Kensington and Chelsea – where nearly-new clothes can be picked up for very little.

→ *British Red Cross Shop* (**G** C3); *Mary's Living and Giving Shop* (**D** A2; also other locations); *Beyond Retro, 110-112 Cheshire St* (**J** A1)

Have a curry

North Indian, modern Indian, pan-Indian, the variety and quality of Indian restaurants in the capital is staggering, from the reasonably priced curry houses of Brick Lane (**J** A1) in the East End to the elaborate cuisine of Cinnamon Club (**A** C4) and Chutney Mary (*St James's St*, **A** B1)

Relax in the park

There's no need to go far to get back to nature: London has parks that are as good as the countryside. Grass stretching away into the distance, leafy glades and huge lakes all beckon you to sit down and relax, or take some exercise either walking, cycling, playing tennis or rowing a boat.

→ *Between May and September take in a show at the Open Air Theatre in Regent's Park* (**E** C1); *or go jogging in Hyde Park* (**E** B6)

Ride a black cab and a double-decker bus

Two iconic London features. After a two-year study of the streets of London, known as 'The Knowledge', taxi drivers (cabbies) have earned the reputation of being the best in the world. Old-fashioned and roomy, their cabs weave skilfully in and out of the traffic. Alternatively, sitting upstairs on a double-decker bus is a cheap and wonderful way to see the city.

→ *The no. 15 bus route uses an original 'Routemaster' double-decker bus from the 1950s: Tower Hill* (**E** C1) *to Trafalgar Square* (**A** C1)

Take afternoon tea

Introduced in the 1800s by the 7th Duchess of Bedford to relieve in-between-meal hunger pangs, afternoon tea remains a grand affair, but mostly in London's historic hotels. A selection of the world's finest teas, served in the best china, comes with freshly made scones and pastries, preserves,

HYDE PARK

HAVE A CURRY

DOUBLE-DECKER BUS

A BEER AT THE PUB

Day trips

WINDSOR CASTLE

DULWICH PICTURE GALLERY

Excursions within 1 hour of the city... plus good places to eat

Kew Gardens

➔ *Kew Rd, Richmond Subway/train to Kew Gardens; Tel. 020 8332 5655 Gardens: Daily 10am– 6.30pm (7.30pm Sat-Sun; 4.15pm in winter) Palace: April-Sep: daily 10am–5.30pm*
These famous gardens were founded in 1759 by the widow of Frederick, Prince of Wales, on the grounds of their summer residence. Over 30,000 varieties of plants from various climates are spread over 300 acres, while the buildings include greenhouses, a Chinese pagoda (1762) and a Dutch-style royal palace (with its interior open to the public).

The Cricketers

➔ *79 Kew Green, Richmond Tel. 020 8940 4372; Fri-Sun noon–11pm (10.30pm Sun)*
The terrace of this delightful pub situated close to Kew Gardens offers ringside views of the local cricket pitch. Entrées £15–20.

Richmond

➔ *Subway/train: Richmond*
This lively, sophisticated suburb is situated by the Thames, which can be crossed via various bridges. Walk to the south to reach the pretty Terrace Gardens and then to Richmond Park, once royal hunting grounds and still home to deer. Take the 371 bus to get back to the subway station.

Hollyhock Café

➔ *Terrace Gardens (between Richmond center and Richmond Park) Tel. 020 8948 6555 Daily 9am–sunset*
Homemade organic food served under a leafy arbor. Entrées £4–6.

Ham House

➔ *Ham St, Richmond Subway/train to Richmond Tel. 020 8940 1950 House: noon–4pm (days depend on the month) Garden: daily 10am–4.30pm*
The ghosts of the Duke and Duchess of Lauderdale are said to haunt the lavish manor they built in the 17th century. Inside, a sculpted wooden staircase, stucco ceilings, gilded wainscoting, leather and silk wall coverings.

The Orangery Café

➔ *In the grounds of Ham House; Tel. 020 8940 1950 Daily 10am–4.30pm*
This enchanting building opposite a scented garden serves healthy vegetable dishes, as well as wonderful cakes. Entrées £5–12.

Hampton Court Palace

➔ *East Molesey, Surrey Train to Hampton Court (from Waterloo station) Tel. 0844 482 7777 Daily 10am–6pm (4.30pm in winter)*
This palace – built around 1514, enlarged by Henry VIII in 1540 and then continually refurbished until the 18th century – was much loved by the royal family. Inside, apartments decorated in Renaissance and baroque style, a sumptuous royal chapel and 16th-century Tudor kitchens. In the

Black cabs
If the orange sign on the roof is illuminated, the taxi is available. Tell the driver where you want to go before getting in.

Minicabs
Cheaper than black cabs; always use a licensed company.

Cabwise
A minicab request service.

→ *Text 'CAB' to 60835 wherever you are in London to receive details of local licenced companies*

Dial a Cab
→ *Tel. 020 7253 5000 (cash bookings) or 7426 3420 (credit cards)*

TAXIS / BLACK CABS

ON THE SUBWAY ('THE UNDERGROUND' OR 'THE TUBE')

TRAIN STATIONS

→ *Tel. 08457 48 49 50 nationalrail.co.uk*
Charing Cross (A D1)
→ *Canterbury, southeast*
Euston (D C3)
→ *Edinburgh, north, northwest*
Liverpool Street (C E3)
→ *Cambridge, east coast*
London Bridge (I D1)
→ *South, southeast*
Paddington (F F1)
→ *Bath, Oxford, west*
King's Cross / St Pancras (D D3)
→ *Edinburgh, Cambridge, north, northeast*
Victoria (A A4)
→ *Brighton, southwest*
Waterloo (H B3)
→ *Dover, south, southwest*

Merlyn Court (G A2)
→ *2 Barkston Gardens, SW5
Tel. 020 7370 1640
merlyncourthotel.com*
A quiet place near Earl's Court Station, with antique furniture in the pleasant rooms, which overlook a pretty square. £100.

La Gaffe (off map **D** A1)
→ *107-111 Heath St, NW3 (Hampstead subway)
Tel. 020 7435 8965
lagaffe.co.uk*
Rustic, family-run hotel in the village setting of Hampstead. Italian restaurant, patio and terrace. £99–129.

Garden Court Hotel (F D1)
→ *30-31 Kensington Gardens Sq, W2; Tel. 020 7229 2553
gardencourthotel.co.uk*
Charming guesthouse run by the same family for the past 60 years. Pretty rooms with flat-screen TVs and a lovely garden. £100–160.

Luna Simone Hotel (A B5)
→ *47-49 Belgrave Rd, SW1
Tel. 020 7834 5897
lunasimonehotel.com*
A well-kept family-run hotel of long standing, with 36 spacious rooms. Efficient, helpful staff. £100–150.

Georgian House Hotel (A A5)
→ *33-35 St George's Drive, SW1; Tel. 020 7834 1438
georgianhousehotel.co.uk*
A charming family-run boutique hotel in a 19th-century house close to Victoria Station. There are two 'Wizard Chambers' complete with four-poster beds and Gothic decor... for Harry Potter fans! £105–160; Wizard Chamber: £269.

Harlingford (D D4)
→ *61-63 Cartwright Gardens, WC1; Tel. 020 7387 1551
harlingfordhotel.com*
Forty-three comfortable

rooms with modern decor, pale wood furniture and full facilities. Also has a bright breakfast room; reasonable prices. From £125–170.

Arran House Hotel (B B1)
→ *77-79 Gower St, WC1
Tel. 020 7636 2186*
Not far from the British Museum, 28 small but well-equipped rooms in a Georgian house. Free Wifi, lounge with sofas and a small garden. £125–175.

Hampstead Village Guesthouse
(off map **D** A1)
→ *2 Kemplay Rd, NW3 (Hampstead subway)
Tel. 020 7435 8679
hampsteadguesthouse.com*
Situated in a pretty street, this nine-room B&B is full of character (one has a free-standing bath tub, another has its own tiny terrace) and filled with books and antiques. There

is a lovely garden where breakfast is served in summer. £105 (shared bathroom)–125. Studio (1–5 people): £125–200.

OVER £150

Amsterdam
(off map **G** A2)
→ *7 Trebovir Rd, SW5
Tel. 020 7370 5084
(Earl's Court subway)
amsterdam-hotel.com*
A homely, peaceful hotel with views over the shady private garden from some of the rooms. £175–195.

The Mad Hatter (H D2)
→ *3-7 Stamford St, SE1
Tel. 020 7401 9222
madhatterhotel.com*
This hotel, set above a Victorian pub, has 30 plush rooms decorated in a contemporary but classic style. Those that give onto the street can be noisy. £170–222.

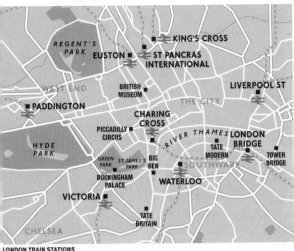

LONDON TRAIN STATIONS

PUBLIC TRANSPORT

Information
→ Tel. 0843 222 1234
tfl.gov.uk
Nine zones (zones 1 and
2 cover central London).
Subway and DLR
→ Mon-Sat 5.30am–
12.30am; Sun 7am–
11.30pm (certain lines
run 24hrs Fri-Sat)
Subway
11 lines
**Docklands Light
Railway (DLR)**
Links the City to the
Docklands / East End.
Trains
→ Daily 5.50am–12.30am
depending on the route;
fewer trains on Sundays
Bus
→ Daily 5am–midnight
Check the destination
displayed on the front.
Night buses
→ Until 5am on some lines
Most go by Trafalgar
Square.
Tickets
Subway and DLR
→ £4.90 single (zones 1-2)
→ £2.40–2.90 (zones 1-2)
per journey with an Oyster
Card (with a daily maximum
cap of £6.50)
Bus
→ £2.40 single (buy tickets
before boarding, from a
machine at the bus stop)
→ £1.50 with an Oyster Card;
1-day pass: £5
Oyster Card
→ £5 deposit; from subway
stations or order online in
advance
Rechargeable subway,
train and bus pass.
London Travelcard
Bus, subway and trains
(within London).
→ £12/one day; £32.10/
one week (zones 1-2)

Boundary (C E1)
→ 2-4 Boundary St, E2
Tel. 020 7729 1051
theboundary.co.uk
This Victorian warehouse-
turned-boutique hotel
celebrates modern design.
Each of the 12 spacious
rooms is devoted to a
different designer: Charles
& Ray Eames, Andrée
Putman, Le Corbusier,
Mies van der Rohe. The
bathrooms alone are
worth a visit; and the
stunning roof terrace
planted with 100 olive
trees has a bar, grill
restaurant and panoramic
views of the city. From
£200–295.

Gir Lion Lodge (D B3)
→ London Zoo Regent's Park
Outer Circle; Tel. 020 7722
3333; May-Sep; zsl.org
A hotel within London
Zoo's lion enclosure.
Guests in the nine
comfortable and brightly
colored wooden cabins

with elegant verandahs
are well protected even
though they are within
roaring distance of the
lions. £378–558 (including
breakfast, dinner and a
visit to the zoo).

LUXURY HOTELS

*Even if you don't stay at one
of these hotels, they are
wonderul places to visit for
a drink or afternoon tea
(usually served 3–5.30pm;
£40–80 with champagne;
reservation advised)*

**St Pancras
Renaissance Hotel
(D D3)**
→ Euston Rd, NW1
Tel. 020 841 3540
stpancrasrenaissance.co.uk
Formerly the Midland
Grand Hotel, this red-brick
High Victorian Gothic
masterpiece (1873) by
Sir George Gilbert Scott
reopened in 2011. It took
ten years and dozens of

craftsmen but the gold-leaf
ceilings, hand-stenciled
wall designs, ironwork and
Europe's grandest double
staircase have been
restored to their original
splendor: 245 rooms and
suites; Melogy barbers;
Victorian tiled pool and
spa; restaurant and two
bars. From £270–300.

The Ritz (A A1)
→ 150 Piccadilly, W1
Tel. 020 7300 2222
theritzlondon.com
World-famous luxury
hotel (opened 1906).
Tea is served in the
spectacular Palm Court.
From £400.

Claridge's (E D4)
→ 49 Brook St, W1
Tel. 020 7629 8860
claridges.co.uk
This Mayfair Art Deco
gem started life as a small
hotel in 1812. Restaurant:
Gordon Ramsay at
Claridge's. Tea is served
in the Foyer. From £480.

clotted cream and dainty finger sandwiches. A glass of champagne is the luxury option.
→ *The Ritz* (**A** A1), *The Orangery* (**F** D3)

Enjoy a drink in a pub
The public house, one of the most characteristic features of English social life, is still a favorite meeting place after work. Many historic pubs have given way to gastropubs, where food gets as much attention as the beer, but there are some fine examples of the old-fashioned pub around.
→ *The Black Friar* (**C** B4); *The Prospect of Whitby, 57 Wapping Wall* (**J** B2); *Ye Olde Cheshire Cheese, 145 Fleet St* (**C** B3); *The Jerusalem Tavern* (**C** B2)

Browse Borough Market (**I** C2)
The oldest food market in London (1756) is a paradise for foodies. Under London Bridge railway arches, behind Southwark Cathedral, fresh food stalls and small stores sell mostly organic produce – herbs and spices, meat, fish, cheese, oils, bread, cakes and much more.
→ *Go early to avoid the late-morning rush*

See a show
There have been theaters and public concerts in London ever since the reign of Henry VIII (1509–47), as witness the reconstructed Globe Theatre (**I** B1), a replica of Shakespeare's own playhouse. The West End (**B**), where 'Theatreland' is centered around the Strand, Piccadilly Circus and Leicester Square, offers a vast choice of plays and musicals. Every summer, the Royal Albert Hall (**G** B1) is home to the BBC Proms, a wonderful season of orchestral and choral music.
→ *Tickets are 50 percent cheaper at the TKTS kiosk in Leicester Square* (**B** C4); *Mon-Sat 10am–7pm; Sun 11am–4.30pm*

The Queen's Walk
The Queen's Walk is a marvelous quayside promenade following the Thames from Lambeth Bridge (**H** A5) to Tower Bridge (**I** F1) passing by popular attractions and famous cultural institutions: the London Eye, the National Theatre, Shakespeare's Globe Theatre, Tate Modern, the Design Museum…To see it all from the water, try one of the pleasure boats that sail from Westminster (**A** D3) to Greenwich (**J** E4).

Go clubbing till dawn
From huge nightclubs to bars with a single dance floor, from frantic rock to classical jazz, London has it all. Soho (**B**), Notting Hill (**F**) and Camden (**D**) have always had a dynamic nightlife, and more recently Islington (**D**), Hoxton and Shoreditch (**C**) have caught up with them.
→ *Fabric* (**C** B2)

…and even when it's raining

Museums
The best time to visit the national museums – and they are free!

Covered markets
Stay dry while shopping inside these 19th-century structures. Covent Garden (**B** D4), Old Spitalfields Market (**C** F2)

Tearooms
Cozy places to take refuge in. Maison Bertaux (**B** C3), Rose Bakery (**E** D5)

Open-air swimming
London Fields Lido (off map **D** F1)
→ *London Fields West Side Subway: London Fields Tel. 020 7254 9038*

Rain is not enough to deter swimmers in this heated open-air pool.

Bowling or table tennis
All Stars Lanes (**B** D2)
→ *Bloomsbury Place Tel. 020 7025 2676* Retro bowling alley in the city center. Bounce (**C** E1)
→ *241 Old St Tel. 020 3657 6525* Table-tennis tables, plus a cocktail bar/restaurant.

Movie theater
Blockbusters and arthouse films at the stunning Picturehouse Central (**B** B4)
→ *Corner of Shaftesbury Ave and Gt Windmill St*

DRESS VINTAGE

BOROUGH MARKET

RICHMOND

EXCURSION SITES

garden is the famous Maze.

Tiltyard Café
→ *In the grounds of Hampton Court Palace*
Tel. 020 3166 6971; Daily 10am–6pm (5pm in winter)
A bright café with sandwiches and hot dishes on offer. Food can also be taken away for a picnic in the gardens. Entrées £5–12.

Windsor Castle
→ *Windsor*
Train to Windsor & Eton Central (from Waterloo station); Tel. 020 7766 7304 March-Oct: daily 9.45am–5.15pm (4.15pm in winter)
The oldest royal castle (1070) contains a thousand rooms, many overlooking the Thames. Its magnificent halls display paintings by Holbein, Rubens and Van Eyck, sculptures by

Gibbons, furniture by Boulle, and the world's largest doll house, built for Queen Mary in 1924.

The Tower Brasserie
→ *The Harte and Garter Hotel & Spa, 31 High St, Windsor; Tel. 0844 855 9131 Mon-Fri 11am–10.30pm; Sat-Sun 8am–11pm*
An elegant little restaurant serving fried fish, curries, game and high tea. Entrées £13.

Warner Bros. Studio Tour (Harry Potter)
→ *Train to Watford Junction (from Euston Station) then the shuttle bus; Tel. 08450 840 900; Daily 10am–6pm (tickets must be booked in advance) wbstudiotour.co.uk*
Hogwarts School and other sets used for the eight Harry Potter films between 2001 and 2011, as well as inside secrets on the filming.

Studio Café
→ *Tel. 08450 840 900 Daily 10am–6.30pm (depending on the season)*
A chance to recover from the excitement of the tour. Serves afternoon tea, with scones and clotted cream.

Dulwich Picture Gallery
→ *Gallery Rd, Dulwich Subway/train to Brixton (from Victoria station), then P4 bus; Tel. 020 8693 5254; Tue-Sun 10am–5pm*
The construction of England's oldest public gallery was entrusted to the architect John Soane, a master of natural light. Dazzling collection of work by old masters from the 16th–18th centuries: Veronese, Poussin, Rembrandt, Hogarth.

Gail's Artisan Bakery
→ *91 Dulwich Village Tel. 020 8693 1787*

Mon-Fri 7am–8pm; Sat-Sun 8am–7pm
Tasty lunches based on savory pies and pastries, plus appetizing salads. Snacks £5–9.

Eltham Palace
→ *Court Yard, Eltham Train to Mottingham (from Charing Cross station) Tel. 020 8294 2548 Sun 10am–4pm*
The wealthy couple Stephen and Virginia Courtauld transformed this 14th-century royal palace into a sophisticated Art-Deco masterpiece and added a Japanese garden.

Eltham Palace Café
→ *Tel. 020 8294 2548 Sun 10am–4pm*
Traditional dishes: soups, sausages & mash, puddings, in a stylish conservatory. Entrées £4–15.

Legend:

- Bakerloo
- Central
- Circle
- District
- Hammersmith & City
- Jubilee
- Metropolitan
- Northern
- Piccadilly
- Victoria
- Waterloo & City
- DLR
- Emirates Air Line
- London Overground
- TfL Rail
- District — open weekends and on some public holidays

- ○ Interchange stations
- Step-free access from street to train
- Step-free access from street to platform
- ⇌ National Rail
- Riverboat services
- Trams
- ✈ Airport
- Victoria Coach Station
- Emirates Air Line

MAYOR OF LONDON

tfl.gov.uk

24 hour travel information
0343 222 1234*

*Service and network charges may apply. See tfl.gov.uk/terms for details.

© Transport for London

Reg. user No. 16/3012/P

Improvement works may

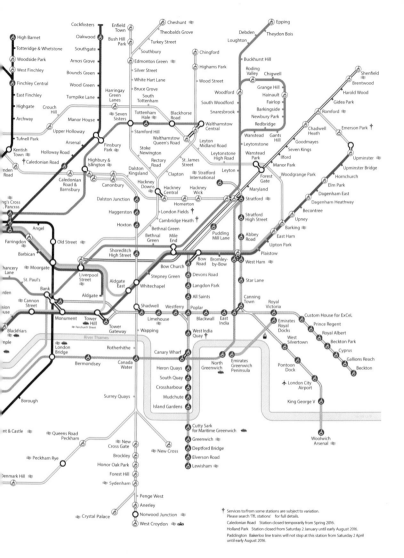

† Services to/from some stations are subject to variation.
Please search 'TfL stations' for full details.
Caledonian Road Station closed temporarily from Spring 2016.
Holland Park Station closed from Saturday 2 January until early August 2016.
Paddington Bakerloo line trains will not stop at this station from Saturday 2 April until early August 2016.

email updates
uk/emailupdates

@TfLTravelAlerts

UNDERGROUND

TRANSPORT
FOR LONDON
EVERY JOURNEY MATTERS

hey, please check before you travel

Version A TfL 01.2016

Correct at time of going to print

The names of streets, monuments and places to visit are followed by a map reference, the first letter of which, in bold (**A, B, C...**), refers to the corresponding area and map. The symbol ✪ refers to the Top Ten sights page at the front of the guide.